MUMBO JUMBO

MUMBO JUMBO

by Robin Glendinning

CHAPPELL PLAYS

LONDON

A member of the Chappell and Intersong Music Group

First published 1987 by
Chappell Plays Ltd,
129 Park Street, London W1Y 3FA

© Copyright Robin Glendinning, 1987

ISBN 0 85676 133 8

Typeset and printed by Commercial Colour Press, London E7.
Cover design by Robin Lowry.

MUMBO JUMBO was first presented at the Royal Exchange Theatre, Manchester, on 8 May 1986, with the following cast:

THE DEAN	Nigel Stock
MRS HOWLETT	Richenda Carey
BILL DUNHAM	Denys Hawthorne
MARION DUNHAM	Anne Lawson
BARRY DUNHAM	Michael Grandage
CREANEY	John Elmes
PATTERSON	Dan Gordon
BROWN	Anthony Hearne
BUTLER	Peter Richey
DUNBAR	Dermott Graham
LOWRY(BOBBY)	David Adair
McKENNA	David Michaels
RICHARDS(WOMBAT)	Marcus O'Higgins
ROBINSON	Maurice Dee
JAMESON	Adam Sunderland or Jason Moss
ANGELA	Sadie Frost

Directed by Nicholas Hytner
Designed by Mark Thompson

The play was subsequently presented at the Lyric Players Theatre, Belfast. The play was premièred in London at the Lyric Theatre, Hammersmith, on 12 May 1987.

For Lorna

CHARACTERS

BARRY DUNHAM	A seventeen-year-old schoolboy
BILL DUNHAM	His father, a High Court Judge
MARION DUNHAM	His mother
THE DEAN	His housemaster (English)
CREANEY	His friend
PATTERSON	Another schoolboy
MRS HOWLETT	The headmaster's wife (English)
JAMESON	Younger schoolboy
ANGELA	A sixteen-year-old girl, neighbour of the Dunhams
BROWN, BUTLER, DUNBAR McKENNA, RICHARDS & LOWRY	Classmates of Barry

The play takes place in a boys' public school in Belfast, in the grounds of the school, in the Dunham's home in suburban Belfast and in the robing room of a High Court Judge.

The time is the present.

The poem spoken by the boys is *The Congo* by the American poet Vachel Lindsay, 1879–1931. (The text of the poem is reprinted in full on pages 100–104.)

NOTE
The set is simple, open and flexible: ideally, desks and furniture which can be wheeled on and off easily. There should be some form of beam, high above the stage, on which actors can perch. The fence can be either permanent or removable. It should be strong enough for Barry to vault over.

photograph by Kevin Cummins from the Manchester Royal Exchange Theatre production of Mumbo Jumbo.

ACT ONE

The DEAN *is seated in front of his class, with a book on his knee. He conducts the class with a walking stick; another stick rests against his chair. Where it says boy, it is unimportant which member of the class says the line.*

DEAN	One, two, three, four!
CLASS	(*chant*) 'Fat black bucks in a wine barrel room...'
BOY	'Barrel-house kings, with feet unstable Sagged and reeled and pounded on the table...'
CLASS	'Pounded on the table!'
BOY	'Beat an empty barrel with the handle of a broom!'
DEAN	Breath, breath!
CLASS	'Hard as they were able BOOM, BOOM, BOOM!'
BOY	'With a silk umbrella and the handle of a broom.'
DEAN	Vowels!
CLASS	'Boomlay, Boomlay, Boomlay, BOOM!'
DEAN	Dunham!
BARRY	'*Then* I had religion, *Then* I had a vision.'
DEAN	Creaney!
CREANEY	'I could not turn from their revel in derision.'
DEAN	Patterson!
PATTERSON	'Then I saw the Congo.'
DEAN	*Consonants!*
CLASS	'Creeping through the black Cutting through the forest with a golden track.'

(*Pause. The* DEAN *has gone rigid, his chin and head thrust forward, eyes staring. It is as if he is in an open-eyed trance. The boys call this condition 'a stare'.*)

BARRY	(*uncertainly*) 'Then along that river bank...'
BUTLER	Shhhhh.
BARRY	'A thousand miles...'
BUTLER	Shut up!
DUNBAR	The Dean's in a stare.
	(*The* CLASS *look at the* DEAN *and wave their arms about. They begin to chant softly.*)
CLASS	The Dean's in a stare, the Dean's in a stare, the Dean's in a stare...
CREANEY	(*over the top of the continuing chant*) Did someone get the clock on him?
LOWRY	I did, I did.
	(*The chanting grows louder.*)
PATTERSON	It's a long one.
CREANEY	What's the record?
BUTLER	(*lifting desk lid and reading paper stuck on the inside*) One minute, twenty-two seconds.
LOWRY	(*timing with watch*) Twenty-two, twenty-three, twenty-four...etc...
	(*The boys' chanting dies away as the* DEAN *comes to. He is now watching* LOWRY *count, concentrating on his watch. The class titters.*)
LOWRY	...thirty four, thirty five etc...
DEAN	What are you doing, boy?
LOWRY	(*startled*) C...c...counting, sir.
DEAN	What are you counting?
LOWRY	S...s...s...seconds, sir.
DEAN	I do assure you that you are going to tire of this before I do. Why are you counting seconds?
BUTLER	(*happy inspiration*) Seconds left till the end of the period, sir.

DEAN	The length of the period may surprise you; that is, it may well extend beyond the span allotted to it in the timetable; that is, until I have your undivided attention. Do I make myself clear?
LOWRY	Yes, sir.
DEAN	Well, what is keeping you?
BARRY	(*dully*) 'A thigh-bone beating on a tin-pan gong.'
DEAN	(*urging*) Everybody!
CLASS	(*without enthusiasm*) ' "Blood" screamed the whistles and the fifes of warriors.'
RICHARDS	(*out of time*) ' "Blood" screamed the skull-faced lean...'
	(*The rest of the class react with disgusted cries of 'Wombat!!'*)
DEAN	STOP! That's no good. Poetry can set you free, especially strongly rhythmical poetry like this; it's a vehicle for developing the vocal possibilities within each of you. You are victims of your environment. That famous Ulster reticence. (*He makes a truly awful attempt at an Ulster accent.*) 'Whatever you say say nothing', ha, ha, ha, ha, ha. Your speech is sloppy, slovenly, dull, restricted, constricted, no freedom, no resonance, not from here. (*He pats his diaphragm.*) You are unaware of your physical powers; they are yours to use...(*Accent again.*) 'If in doubt say nowt'. Ha, ha, ha, ha, ha. Right relax, breathe in, from here...(*waves his stick.*)
RICHARDS	(*magnificently*) ' "BLOOD" screamed the skull-faced lean witch-doctors.'
BARRY	'Whirl ye the deadly voodoo rattle.'
BOY	'Harry the uplands.'
BOY	'Steel all the cattle.'

DEAN	'Rattle-rattle, rattle-rattle.'
BOY	Bing.
CLASS	'Boomlay, boomlay, boomlay, boom!'
	(*The school bell rings.*)
DEAN	Dismissed. Dunham!
	(BARRY *goes to the* DEAN *and they talk upstage as the* CLASS *wheels off the desks.*)
CREANEY	He's finally flipped his lid.
RICHARDS	I think it's great.
DUNBAR	Wombat thinks it's great.
ALL	Shut up, Wombat.
DUNBAR	If you think it's so bloody good, you get up on Founders' Day on your *own* and do it.
RICHARDS	Well, it's more of an ensemble piece.
ALL	Ohhhhh!
PATTERSON	Come on, Wombat. Give us a critical appreciation of this poem.
DUNBAR	Yeah. Give us a literary interpretation of 'bing'.
LOWRY	Yeah. Give us a literary interpretation of 'bing'.
RICHARDS	You can't just take a word out of context.
BUTLER	Dunbar, I wouldn't do it.
DUNBAR	Do what?
RICHARDS	Especially a word like 'bing'.
CREANEY	Not costumes.
DUNBAR	What costumes?
BUTLER	You know he did this four years ago. They've still got the costumes. He wears khaki shorts and a pith helmet and whoever leads it wears a grass skirt and beats it out on a drum.
CREANEY	Someone with good rhythm.

(Pause.)

McKenna   That's you Dunbar. All your Paisley marches.

ALL   Ooooooh.

DUNBAR   What the fuck would you know about Paisley marches?

LOWRY   What the fuck would you know about Paisley marches, McKenna?

DUNBAR   Well said, Bobby, see ya Mick.

(All the desks have now been removed. The DEAN makes a funny little run forward, moving with short, fast steps, as though involuntary. At the same time he grimaces, chin thrust forward, shoulders hunched, his elbows sticking into his side and his hands flicking outwards. The boys call this involuntary run forward a 'shoot' and the spasmodic jerk of the arms a 'flick'. The DEAN's spasm passes and he is able to make a dignified exit with the aid of his sticks. BARRY, CREANEY and PATTERSON have remained on stage, watching him go.)

CREANEY   *(imitating, cruelly)* Flick!

PATTERSON   *(likewise)* Shoot!

CREANEY
PATTERSON   *(chanting together)* Shoot flick the Dean, shoot flick the Dean.

(They imitate the grotesque little movements, laughing. BARRY watches in silence.)

CREANEY   What in hell makes the silly old bugger do that?

PATTERSON   *(knowledgeably)* Oh it's undoubtedly a nervous tic of some kind; a sort of minor neurasthenic disorder.

CREANEY   *(impressed)* Wow!

PATTERSON   I intend to take up medicine.

CREANEY   What about the stare?

PATTERSON   Petit Mal.

CREANEY	What?
PATTERSON	A mild form of epilepsy.
CREANEY	I thought he fell out of a spitfire without a parachute.
PATTERSON	Not inconsistent with those particular symptoms.
CREANEY	He's supposed to have a steel plate in his skull.
PATTERSON	Probably producing pressure on his frontal lobes.
CREANEY	Boring old fart.
PATTERSON	Shoot.
CREANEY	Flick.
PATTERSON CREANEY	} *(together)* Stare!

(*They both end up staring at* BARRY.)

PATTERSON	We're offending Dunham.
CREANEY	Poor old Dum Dum's offended.
BARRY	If he fell out of a spitfire he was serving his country.
CREANEY	(*pityingly*) Oh Dum Dum's offended.
PATTERSON	Of course you know why.
CREANEY	We have offended Dum Dum.
PATTERSON	The Dean fancies him.

(CREANEY *gives a salacious laugh.*)

PATTERSON	That's why he picked him for Hamlet.
BARRY	I auditioned!
PATTERSON	He asked you to audition, he pleaded with you to audition!
BARRY	I wanted to audition!
CREANEY	You should have heard what the Dean said to him at lights out.

PATTERSON	What?
BARRY	Shut up, Creaney.
PATTERSON	Go on, go on.
BARRY	You bloody well know it was a joke.
PATTERSON	What did the Dean say to his darling Dunners?
BARRY	It was an effing joke!
CREANEY	'Good night sweet prince.'
BARRY	It was a frigging joke for Christ's sake!
PATTERSON	(*laughing*) I should watch out Dunners, if I were you.
BARRY	Why?
PATTERSON	No little approaches at rehearsals?
BARRY	Ach, come off it Patterson!
CREANEY	He's got to get his pleasure some way.
PATTERSON	No friendly hand on the shoulder?
BARRY	(*firmly*) No!
CREANEY	Unless the fall from the spitfire did for that as well.
PATTERSON	No fluttering of the fingertips around your tight little rear?
BARRY	No, no, no!
	(*Pause.*)
PATTERSON	'Methinks he doth protest too much.'
CREANEY	No smoke without fire.
BARRY	You're both disgusting.
CREANEY	Why Dum Dum?
BARRY	Sewer rats!
PATTERSON	But why Dunners?
BARRY	All you ever talk about is sex!
PATTERSON	But sex is not disgusting Dunners, is it Creaney?

CREANEY	No.
PATTERSON	Sex is beautiful. Isn't sex beautiful, Creaney?
CREANEY	Magic.
PATTERSON	The Reverend Brian Morrison says it's only those who have an unhealthy and unwholesome attitude to sex that think it is disgusting. He says that the sniggerers and the smutty talkers just reveal their lack of maturity.
CREANEY	Do you lack maturity, Dum Dum?
BARRY	I wasn't sniggering.
PATTERSON	You did mention sewer rats.
BARRY	Bloody hell, it was you two...
PATTERSON	You should come to his talks.
BARRY	...it was you two who were doing all the sniggering.
PATTERSON	'Sex and the modern Christian.'
CREANEY	Don't take it to heart, Dum Dum.
BARRY	I am not taking it to heart!
PATTERSON	At the Christian Union every Tuesday.
CREANEY	(*trying to make peace*) Alright, Dum Dum, alright.
BARRY	It was you!
PATTERSON	The Reverend Brian Morrison is very explicit.
CREANEY	(*sudden interest*) Explicit?
PATTERSON	Take you out of yourself, Dunham.
BARRY	I do not need taking out of myself.
PATTERSON	Cure you of your self-obsession.
BARRY	I am not self-obsessed!
PATTERSON	You could have fooled me.
BARRY	Bugger off!
PATTERSON	Charming.

BARRY	Fuck off!
PATTERSON	Language like that shows a lack of imagination.
BARRY	(*threatening*) I'll kick the shit out of you, Patterson!
PATTERSON	(*exiting*) Especially in someone who has pretensions to be a poet.

(*Pause.* BARRY *seethes.*)

CREANEY	Forget that supercilious bastard.
BARRY	You sided with him!
CREANEY	No, I didn't.
BARRY	With him against me!
CREANEY	It was a joke.
BARRY	I asked you not to tell him that.
CREANEY	Oh, for God's sake, don't take it so seriously. It was a joke. Anyway, you were defending that old cripple.
BARRY	I don't give a damn about...(*without conviction*)...the old fart.
CREANEY	You *have* entered his precious poetry competition.
BARRY	Yes.
CREANEY	Clouds and daffodils?
BARRY	No.
CREANEY	Won't win then!
BARRY	What the hell do you know about it?
CREANEY	Unless, of course, it's leech-gatherers or nutters!
BARRY	Look, you great cretin, poetry can be tough and hard and honest and true. In fact, it's no bloody good if it isn't.
CREANEY	Has nobody told you the rules, Dum Dum?

BARRY	What rules?
CREANEY	To succeed as a poet in this country you have to be called Seamus.
BARRY	You are a typical thick Prod, aren't you?
CREANEY	(*truculently*) Yeah!
BARRY	No shame!
CREANEY	None. Just hard and honest and true.
BARRY	(*laughs*) OK...Look, the Dean may have old-fashioned ideas, but he's good at technique. I value that. And he tries to encourage me.
CREANEY	He tries to discourage me.
BARRY	I've never heard him discourage anyone.
CREANEY	He called me Neanderthal man; that's pretty discouraging.
BARRY	A joke.
CREANEY	Bloody funny joke, to be told you have one of the finest minds of the early Stone Age.
BARRY	You deserved it.
CREANEY	Why?
BARRY	You make such stupid bloody statements.
CREANEY	Like?
BARRY	Oh for goodness sake, you told him that the battle of the Boyne was the turning point in world history.
CREANEY	What's wrong with that?
BARRY	Ach, come off it.
CREANEY	It was a turning point.
BARRY	Of world history? The greatest thing from the decline and fall of the Roman Empire to the rise of Mao Tse Tung?
CREANEY	Well, I admit it hadn't a big impact on China.
BARRY	It was of minor European importance.

CREANEY	The Pope was pleased enough.
BARRY	You don't have to justify your bigotry to me.
CREANEY	It wasn't bigotry.
BARRY	What was it then?
CREANEY	I wasn't going to let an Englishman make light of the whole thing as if it didn't matter whether it had happened or not.
BARRY	He was laughing at you.
CREANEY	I don't care.
BARRY	He thinks you're a buffoon.
CREANEY	Does he? (*Half a smile.*)
BARRY	Of course he does.
CREANEY	(*half a laugh*) Oul shite.
BARRY	Buffooooooooooooooon!
CREANEY	If he wants to treat me like a paddy I'll act like a paddy. Jesus, I'll buffoon the bastard.
	(*They both laugh quietly.*)
CREANEY	Hey?
BARRY	What?
CREANEY	What about the God squad then? Sex and the modern Christian? Do you think we should? This hell hole would put the bloody mockers on you. (*Pause.*) I need a girl, Dum Dum. I need a girl very soon, if I don't get a girl soon...Jackson got it you know.
BARRY	What?
CREANEY	The narles.
BARRY	Oh.
CREANEY	You know that piece that hangs around the side gate?
BARRY	No.
CREANEY	Yes you do.

BARRY	No I don't.
CREANEY	Red face. Big knockers. Fat legs. Wears a wet-look mini skirt stretched tight over her bum. I've seen you watching her.
BARRY	No you haven't!
	(*Pause.*)
CREANEY	Alright Dum Dum, I haven't. I have though.
BARRY	I may have caught sight of her.
CREANEY	You were staring.
BARRY	From a distance.
CREANEY	Your eyes were on stair rods.
BARRY	Briefly.
CREANEY	She was flirting with three third formers and you were standing there looking on and wishing like hell it was you.
BARRY	Look, I admit I saw her, once, briefly, from a distance as I was passing.
	(*Pause.*)
CREANEY	Well, Jackson had her twice in one afternoon, lucky get. I'll die if I don't get it soon. The narles. The narly, narly, narles. (*He moans.*) Oh Dum Dum, that big juicy bitch. Can you imagine it, Dum Dum?
BARRY	I've never even kissed a girl.
CREANEY	You're not serious?
BARRY	Not properly; not on the lips, not a real kiss.
CREANEY	Kissing's nothing, Dum Dum.
BARRY	I've never done it.
CREANEY	It's usually them that decides.
BARRY	Is it?
CREANEY	Oh yeah. The first girl I kissed was big Sadie Thompson. Parish social. She asked me into

the cloakroom to see her new prayer book. I thought it a bit odd at the time; I mean big Sadie and prayer books were not what you expected, but I went out of curiosity and as soon as I shut the door she grabbed me. Do you not know any girls, Dum Dum?

BARRY   There's the girl next door.

CREANEY   Kiss her.

BARRY   Her family have just moved in.

CREANEY   If the old man hadn't made so much money dealing and sent me to board in this kip, there's no telling what big Sadie might have done for me by now.

BARRY   I saw her in the garden on the last day of half-term.

CREANEY   Big Sadie's probably had the whole of the temperance flute band by now.

BARRY   She goes to a day school.

CREANEY   Played a tune on each one of them.

BARRY   I'll kiss her.

CREANEY   As far as I'm concerned she can play 'The Protestant Boys' and 'The Green Grassy Slopes of the Boyne' on my flute any time she wants and the sooner the bloody better. She can even play 'Kevin Barry' if she fucking feels like it, but of course she wouldn't. True blue, big Sadie.

BARRY   She was in her school uniform, green skirt, white socks, white shirt and a band in her hair.

CREANEY   I told you you were a goggler, Dum Dum.

BARRY   I happen to be writing a poem about her.

CREANEY   Goggler!

(*The class assembles wheeling on a props basket.* CREANEY *joins them.* BARRY *is left on his own, isolated.*)

RICHARDS	(*trying on a mask from basket*) Hallooo...
DUNBAR	Put a sock in it, Wombat.
BUTLER	I thought you were refusing to do this anyway, Dunbar.
DUNBAR	I am. I'm not doing it.
BUTLER	The girls from Richmond Lodge will enjoy it.
DUNBAR	What?
CREANEY	Yeah. They come every Founders' Day.
RICHARDS	Anyone want a rattle?
ALL	Fuck off, Wombat.
DUNBAR	Well then, I am definitely not doing it.
	(*The* DEAN *enters and starts the poem.*)
CLASS	'Then I heard the boom of the blood-lust song
	And a thigh-bone beating on a tin-pan gong.
	And "BLOOD" screamed the whistles and the fifes of the warriors.
	"BLOOD" screamed the skull-faced, lean witch-doctors,
	"Whirl ye the deadly voo-doo rattle,
	Harry the uplands,
	Steal all the cattle,
	Rattle-rattle, rattle-rattle,
	Bing.
	Boomlay, boomlay, boomlay, BOOM.'
BOY	'A roaring epic rag-time tune
	From the mouth of the Congo
	To the Mountains of the Moon.
BOY	'Death is an Elephant
	Torch-eyed and terrible.'
CLASS	'BOOM.'
DEAN	'Steal the pygmies.'
CLASS	'BOOM.'
DEAN	'Kill the Arabs.'
CLASS	'BOOM.'
DEAN	'Kill the white men.'

CLASS	'HOO, HOO, HOO!'
BARRY	(*attempting to compose a poem in the midst of the chanting*) Poem on a girl. Poem on a girl in the garden. A garden of the mind. Girl in a whirl, the whirl of a skirt...skirt...flirt...swing of a racquet, dance...dance...song of her...feet...feet...Swing ring zing...lilt...A girl in a garden, in the garden...
FIRST BOY	(*simultaneous to* BARRY'S *poem but very much in the background*)
	'Listen to the yell of Leopold's ghost, Burning in Hell for his hand-maimed host.'
SECOND BOY	'Hear how the demons chuckle and yell Cutting his hands off down in Hell.'
DEAN	'Listen to the creepy proclamations.'
FIRST BOY	'Blown through the lairs of the forest nation.'
SECOND BOY	'Blown past the white-ant's hills of clay,'
THIRD BOY	'Blown past the marsh where the butterflies play.'
DEAN	Be careful what you do.
CLASS	'Or Mumbo Jumbo, God of the Congo,'
DEAN	'And all of the other Gods of the Congo,'
	(BARRY *joins the class.*)
CLASS	'Mumbo Jumbo will hoo-doo you Mumbo Jumbo will hoo-doo you Mumbo Jumbo will hoo-doo you.'
	(*The bell rings and the class disperses leaving the* DEAN *and* BARRY.)
DEAN	Dunham?
BARRY	Yes, sir.
DEAN	Mrs Howlett is coming here.
BARRY	Oh yes, sir.
DEAN	So we should wait.

BARRY	Yes, sir.
	(*Pause.*)
DEAN	Did you enjoy the poem?
BARRY	Yes, sir.
DEAN	Rhythmically exciting.
BARRY	Yes, sir.
DEAN	You think it will grace Founder's Day?
BARRY	Yes, sir.
DEAN	(*stepping close to him*) Turn round.
	(BARRY *turns. The* DEAN *places both hands on his ribs at the back.*) Now…let me feel the ribs move when you breathe in.
	(BARRY *breathes deeply.*)
	'Mumbo Jumbo will hoo-doo you'
BARRY	(*as he breathes out*) 'Mumbo Jumbo will hoo-doo you'
	(*Pause.*)
DEAN	Be careful what you dooooooooo…(*He laughs.*)
	(BARRY *moves away.*)
	I've read your poem.
BARRY	Oh.
DEAN	It's very good.
BARRY	Thank you.
DEAN	Easily the best.
BARRY	Oh.
DEAN	'The time is out of joint.' Well, you are not the first to employ the predicament of the Prince of Denmark to our own purpose but I venture to guess that it has not often been applied to the Ulster problem.
BARRY	Yes, you see, sir, something is rotten in the State of Denmark, or Ulster; and Hamlet is expected to put it right, and he doubts his own ability, his…

DEAN	Look Dunners, old chap. I have just one caveat, one slight criticism...
BARRY	The metre, I was a bit worried about...
DEAN	I found your pessimism arch—
BARRY	Arch?
DEAN	Forced—
BARRY	Forced?
DEAN	For effect only.
BARRY	But sir, the situation in Northern Ireland is...
DEAN	(*reading the poem*)

'I walk the streets with fear alive,
I stare at the hills with hate ringed round.
The politicians roar and strive
As the blood of victims sours the ground.'

BARRY	I thought those lines were true.
DEAN	Negative. They are negative, aren't they?
BARRY	Well, yes.
DEAN	Well, say something positive. It's so easy being negative, isn't it?
BARRY	Yes, I suppose...
DEAN	Say something positive, about yourself, your times, your province; you do think positively, don't you?
BARRY	Yes, sir.
DEAN	Good. Good. (*Chuckling.*) You do not believe, I take it, that the battle of the Boyne was the most important military engagement in the history of the world?
BARRY	No, sir.
DEAN	Good. Good. (*Pause.*) It is not, you understand, that I am opposed to the expression of strongly held opinions. Good God, most of the boys I come into contact with

express no opinions at all; but I cannot abide that sort of goonery, Dunham, that parochial arrogance bordering on the wilfully stupid. That is what is wrong with Ulster, isn't it? No one else in the world understands us! No one else in the world is like us! We are the great misunderstood of the twentieth century! It is so annoying when people are trying to help. As for the lack of generosity, the refusal to see the other fellow's point of view, the insistence that every mention of compromise is some sort of sell-out. I find that very frustrating; don't you?

BARRY   Yes, sir.

DEAN   So you are a moderate, Dunham?

BARRY   Well a sort of non-militant moderate, sir.

DEAN   I should have thought those two terms were mutually exclusive Dunham.

BARRY   They are, sir, that's the trouble.

DEAN   What trouble?

BARRY   You have no...no cutting edge, sir...in the middle...no certainty...not like...well...(*He tails off.*)

DEAN   Like Creaney?

BARRY   He's a friend of mine, sir, but...well yes.

DEAN   Look, don't get me wrong, I'm very fond of Creaney; according to the maths department he is one of the brightest boys in the class. It's just that he exhibits a certain rustic vulgarity in speech and political outlook. But you stick to your guns, Dunham, you stick to your guns.

BARRY   Yes, sir.

DEAN   (*handing him the poem*) Well, take your poem and think about that final stanza; it has won anyway, but I would like you to try further.

BARRY   Thank you, sir.

Mrs Howlett	(*sweeping in with costume and work bag*) Hello, Dean.
Dean	Mrs Howlett, your feminine charm is most welcome in the austerity of our school hall.
Mrs Howlett	You know very well, Dean, the boys call me the old bat.
Dean	The boys are famous for their lack of taste, Mrs Howlett.
Mrs Howlett	Now master Dunham, just hold this up against your manly torso and let us see if it fits.

(*She tries out the top half of* Barry's *Hamlet costume for size.*)

Dean	Infamous I should say.
Mrs Howlett	Now the legs. 'Old Bat.' Isn't that right, mon chère Dunham?
Barry	No, Mrs Howlett.
Mrs Howlett	Don't lie to me, mon brave. Remember I have taken your inside leg measurements and you cannot lie to someone familiar with your inside leg. Here, put it on, will you? (*Pause as* Barry *shows some reluctance.*) Oh go on Dunham, don't be shy—I'm not asking you to strip to the skin.
Dean	Dunham is a moderate, Mrs Howlett.
Mrs Howlett	Are you, Dunham?
Barry	Yes, Mrs Howlett.
Mrs Howlett	Oh good, I hate it when I can't stand the opinion of boys I like and I like you, Dunham, even when you lie, especially when you lie. Oh Dunham, I'll turn my back. My God, Dean, they are so shy! It's their mothers I blame. You should have seen poor Ophelia when I gave her one of Daphne's bras; otherwise they look so flat chested you know. Well, I handed the poor child this exotic piece of apparatus and he looked up at me with his big puppy

eyes as if to say 'Mrs Howlett, what do I do with this *thing?*' I said to him, 'Jameson mein liebling, you make a sling out of it and hurl rocks at the headmaster's greenhouse.' (DEAN *laughs.*) Do you know I think he believed me. (*He laughs again.*) Turn round Dunham mon tresor. Mmm. It's the legs, isn't it?

DEAN   His legs are rather...

MRS HOWLETT   Thin. Dunham, why aren't your legs fatter?

DEAN   His feet look so big.

MRS HOWLETT   Oh my God yes, his feet. Dean, where do they get such monstrous feet? I keep saying to the headmaster, 'Howlie, why do you take boys with gargantuan feet?' Howlie claims they are better in the scrums. My God, you should see Ophelia's feet! Take it off, Dunham, and I'll have another go. (BARRY *complies.*) Your father is to make the speech on Founder's Day, I believe.

BARRY   Yes, Mrs Howlett.

MRS HOWLETT   When does he take his seat on the bench?

BARRY   Next Wednesday, Mrs Howlett.

MRS HOWLETT   Bill Dunham is the eleventh old boy to be made a Judge, Dean.

DEAN   So I believe.

MRS HOWLETT   Howlie's so pleased he's pouring out the best sherry in bucketfuls to anyone prepared to listen to him on the subject of the school's tradition of service to the community. I tell you, it's almost boring. You must be very, very proud of him, Dunham.

BARRY   Yes, Mrs Howlett.

MRS HOWLETT   He was head boy here, wasn't he?

BARRY   Yes, Mrs Howlett:

MRS HOWLETT   Will you be head boy, Dunham?

BARRY	I don't think so, Mrs Howlett.
MRS HOWLETT	Oh, don't be so negative, Dunham. (*Gathering up the costumes.*) Dean, come over to school house and we'll see if Howlie is still active with that bottle.
DEAN	(*going with* MRS HOWLETT) Not only charm but hospitality as well, Mrs Howlett.
MRS HOWLETT	(*going*) You are an old flatterer, Dean.
DEAN	A batchelor's privilege, dear lady, a batchelor's privilege...

(*They both exit. With a yell of triumph* BARRY's *classmates rush on him.*)

BARRY	Ach, come on boys!

(*They grab his trousers and throw them to each other, shouting and whooping.* BARRY *waits unperturbed.*)

BOY	The old bat fancies Dunham.
BOY	Took his trousers off.
BOY	Dunham fancies the old bat...

(BARRY *grabs* BUTLER *and his trousers.*)

BUTLER	(*into* BARRY's *face*) The old bat give you a feel, Dunham?
BARRY	Typical of you, Butler.
BUTLER	(*truculently*) What is?
BARRY	All the wit and charm of the Newtownards Road.

(*They* ALL *laugh.*)

BUTLER	(*belligerently*) What's wrong with the Newtownards Road?
BARRY	I spoke of its charm and wit. (*Appealing to the others.*) Didn't I say it had wit and charm?
ALL	Yes. Yes...
BUTLER	(*furious*) Shut up about it! (*He breaks away as others laugh at him.*)

BARRY	Anyway, it isn't me the old bat fancies.
BOY	Who is it?
BARRY	Wombat.
RICHARDS	Me?
ALL	Wombat. Wombat.
PATTERSON	Lucky old Wombat.
RICHARDS	Why?
PATTERSON	Experienced women know a thing or two, don't they, Creaney?
CREANEY	Oh yes.
RICHARDS	Seriously?
PATTERSON	Oh yes.
BARRY	She told me she likes to see you togged out in your rugby kit.
RICHARDS	Wow!
BARRY	It's the yellow stockings. (*Moves close to him.*) Cross-gartered.

(*The clever ones in the class laugh.*)

RICHARDS	But they're blue.

(CREANEY *makes another grab for* BARRY'*s trousers. They fight and the rest chant 'Fight Fight' and encircle them.*)

CLASS	'Be careful what you do, Or Mumbo Jumbo, God of the Congo, And all of the other Gods of the Congo, Mumbo Jumbo will hoo-doo you, Mumbo Jumbo will hoo-doo you'

(CREANEY *wins and rolls off Dunham.*)

RICHARDS	(*as they leave*) My socks are blue. The school socks are blue and white stripes, not yellow.
CLASS	(*as they leave taking basket with them*) Oh shut up, Wombat!

CREANEY   Hey, boys, did you hear Jackson got the narles
               again? In Long Field.

PATTERSON   He wants to watch himself.

CREANEY   There isn't a hall of mirrors in Long Field.

PATTERSON   The Reverend Brian Morrison's third lecture
               in his series on sex and the modern Christian
               was about venereal disease. He called it
               'Visiting the sins of the fathers unto the third
               and fourth generation.' He illustrated it with
               coloured slides. Robinson fainted. Well, it was
               pretty gory actually but I managed to preserve
               a sense of clinical detachment which quite
               pleased me in the circumstances. I mean how
               does one know how one will react in such a
               situation until one has experienced it?

               (BARRY *is slowly getting dressed.*)

CREANEY   What else does he lecture about?

PATTERSON   His last talk was about the bounds of decency.

CREANEY   What the hell are they?

PATTERSON   He suggested a formula. H3K2F1.

CREANEY   What does it mean?

PATTERSON   Well, H is holding hands. You can hold hands
               as long as you like; H3, maximum, you see. In
               the Reverend Brian Morrison's phrase, holding
               hands is an 'open and wholesome
               demonstration of affection and regard,
               consistent with chastity'. K. Kissing is more
               complex, naturally. K1, on the lips, OK. K2,
               open mouth acceptable but only between long-
               standing partners. K3, mutual lingual
               exploration, to be avoided until formal
               engagement.

CREANEY   What about F?

PATTERSON   Permissible fully clothed with the lights on.

CREANEY   What?

PATTERSON   Fondling the breast.

CREANEY	Oh.
PATTERSON	F1, a light touching or brief fondling with the tips of the fingers, OK. F2, medium fondling, cupping the breast with an open hand, that's out, so is F3, heavy fondling, kissing or sucking.
CREANEY	What about the bum?
PATTERSON	The buttocks and all other erotic zones are out of bounds until after marriage, in a church, the marriage that is. I have no wish to brag but I think I can congratulate myself that I have stayed within the bounds of decency consistent with chastity. It is comforting that one knew instinctively how far not to go; and how far to go, of course.
CREANEY	Wouldn't want to miss out on that.
PATTERSON	Well naturally I don't claim any sort of credit; it's more of a moral sixth sense. Mind you, I have been tempted. Oh, yes. Once or twice. Pretty little things sending all sorts of signals. Talk about body language. I must confess to a touch of F2 once but I had been going steady for several months and I knew the girl's mother frightfully well; as a matter of fact, just between you and me and the gatepost I suspect she approved, the mother I mean.
CREANEY	Why?
PATTERSON	Well, her daughter was a shy little thing, a mouse really, and I brought her out of herself. Kept asking me round for tea and leaving the two of us together. God, the cake I had to eat; cream flans, Black Forest gateaux, chocolate sponges, raspberry, cherry, my God that woman must have spent all her spare time baking. Well, of course once I got the little mouse going she wanted more, and more. Well, you know what girls are like, especially a reformed mouse.
CREANEY	What happened?

PATTERSON	Well, on this particular evening she was wearing a 'Youth for Christ' T shirt and I was indulging in a bit of tentative F1, on an experimental basis, and I discovered that...*she wasn't wearing a bra!* I must say she did have exquisite breasts. I noticed that. Aesthetically beautiful, for even then you know, I was able to preserve a sort of scientific calm, with part of my brain, it's the observer in me I think. Well, I mean I must have been still in control of myself, mustn't I?
CREANEY	Why?
PATTERSON	To notice their beauty. The breasts.
CREANEY	(*perplexed*) Oh.
PATTERSON	The poor little thing cried like a drain when I told her it would all have to end. Well, I couldn't get too deeply involved, not if I'm going to become a brain surgeon, so I just had to be cruel to be kind. I must admit she was awfully keen on me and of course so was her mother. Keeps asking me round and it's such a bore to have to keep thinking up new excuses. Well, must be going. If you two are interested the next talk is 'Contraception and the Christian conscience.' (*He exits.*)
CREANEY	Bastard. Why the hell have I never fondled the breasts of a girl in a 'Youth for Christ' T shirt? It wouldn't have been on her long if it had been me. Why do they go in for creeps like that? Why? Is God some sort of pervert? Do you know, Dum Dum, I think women are thick. Imagine pulling your 'Youth for Christ' T shirt over your bra-less aesthetically beautiful breasts for that creeping Jesus!
BARRY	I'm going home next Wednesday.
CREANEY	I wish I was.
BARRY	I'm going to kiss the girl next door, really kiss her. K12345 and 6.

CREANEY	Which girl is that, Dum Dum?
BARRY	The one I told you about.
CREANEY	Listen, if you get within half a mile of her, give her a touch of one hundred and twenty-five from me.
BARRY	I'll kiss her in the garden where she plays swing ball.
CREANEY	I think I'll go down the side gate, you never know. Coming?
BARRY	No.
CREANEY	See ya. (*He exits.*)
	(BARRY *moves to centre stage. Lights come up on the swing ball pole and tennis ball. The girl as described by* BARRY *enters and starts to play, hitting the ball forehand and backhand so that it keeps its position on the pole.*)
BARRY	(*watching, for this is still in his mind, he returns to the poem as she plays*) Poem on a girl in a garden of the mind. Feet...dancing, legs twisting, body turning, pivot, swing...swing, swing, swing. Hair. Hair swinging. Head. Chin. Eyes. Lips. Kiss Kissssss. Tongue. Tongue. Tongue. Tongue. Touch...Teeth. Touch. Teeeeeethhh. Breath. Breathinggggggggggggggggg. (*An almost silent cry of despair.*) Oh Godddddd. (*Light fades on girl and comes up on* CLASS *wheeling on desks.*)
DUNBAR	I'd been off sick and instead of popping the thermometer in my mouth she came and sat on the bed.
BOY	God, no.
DUNBAR	'How are you feeling, Jonathan?', she said.
BOY	What did you say?
DUNBAR	I said fine and she said 'Good', and started unzipping her dress.

Boy	Go on.
Dunbar	She took it off.
Boy	And?
Dunbar	And her bra. And her slip. And all the rest. And she pulled back the sheets and got in beside me.
Boy	What happened?
Dunbar	The bloody bell went for reveille and I woke up.
Boy	Bad luck.
Dunbar	Best bloody dream I ever had ruined by the bell.
Richards	Happened to me last week.
Dunbar	No, it didn't.
Richards	How the hell do you know?
Dunbar	It's never happened to you, Wombat!
	(*The* Dean *has entered and he starts the chant.* Barry *has taken his place.*)
Class	'Just then from the doorway, as fat as shotes Came the cake-walk princes in their long red coats, Canes with a brilliant lacquer shine, And tall silk hats that were as red as wine.'
First Boy	'And they pranced with their butterfly partners there Coal-black maidens with curls in their hair, Knee-skirts trimmed with jassamine sweet, And bells on their ankles and little black-feet.'
Second Boy	'And the couples railed at the chant and frown Of the witch-men lean, and laughed them down. (Oh, rare was the revel, and well worth while That made those glowering witch-men smile.)
Third Boy	'The cake-walk royally then began'

FIRST BOY	'To walk for a cake as tall as a man'
SECOND BOY	'To the tune of…'
CLASS	'Boomlay, boomlay, BOOM.'
THIRD BOY	'While the witch-men laughed with a sinister air And sang with the scalawags prancing there;'
FIRST BOY	'Walk with care, walk with care, Or Mumbo Jumbo, God of the Congo,'
CLASS	'Mumbo Jumbo will hoo-doo you.'
SECOND BOY	'Beware, beware, walk with care.'
CLASS	'Boomlay, boomlay, boomlay, boom. Boomlay, boomlay, boomlay, BOOM!'
THIRD BOY	'Oh, rare was the revel, and well worth while That made those glowering witch-men smile.' (*Pause.*)
DEAN	Well done, boys, well done. (*Chuckling*) Do you know what it reminds me of, boys? (*The attempted accent again*) The Twalth! (*Laughs*) 'The Twalth Day of July as it yearly did come' The Walk. 'Cake-walk princes as fat as shotes.' Does that not remind you of the average (*accent*) Grand Master of the local Orange Lodge, eh? (*Some of the boys laugh.*) Certainly reminds me.
CREANEY	(*coolly belligerent*) Why, sir?
DEAN	Oh, Creaney, I think all the colour, the big drums, the bands, the sashes, the regalia, the banners, black bowlers, all that rhythm and ritual, and the witch-doctors too: I think they are not dissimilar.
CREANEY	(*losing cool*) Nothing like it.
DEAN	It is not anything like it, or it is not in the least like it, sir.
CREANEY	It is not in the least like it, *sir!*
DEAN	Surely I don't detect a note of belligerence in that assertion, Creaney? If we have aught to

say we should exercise our powers of logic as well as practising correct syntax? Yes?

CREANEY   The Twelfth of July is the annual commemoration of the battle of the Boyne, sir. The battle of the Boyne was the decisive battle in the glorious revolution which gave us our freedom, religion and laws and it has nothing to do with witch-doctors, sir.

DEAN   Your own obsession with this obscure date in history, Creaney, suggests very strongly that it has, or with the modern equivalent of a witch-doctor. I was making a joke, Creaney. The Ulsterman is famous for his sense of humour, is he not? It's just that he doesn't always see it when he is the butt. Joke Creaney? All right? Just a little (*Accent.*) Just a wee joke, eh?

            (*During the exchanges the* CLASS *react, mainly laughing with the* DEAN *at* CREANEY'S *expense, particularly* McKENNA. DUNBAR *remains on* CREANEY'S *side.*)

CREANEY   Put it in a sentence, sir.

DEAN   I see. I have offended you, Creaney. I assure you that I had no such intention. You must not take offence so easily. Nevertheless I apologise. (*Pause.*) Your challenge, even if it was a trifle intemperate, was a fair one. I will, if I may, use several sentences; all, I hope, with the correct syntax. (*Pause.*) The annual parades on the twelfth day of July are a colourful spectacle, a fascinating and energetic folk festival which does, I concede, celebrate an important event in the development of the British constitution on which our freedom, religion and laws do depend. But there are elements in this quaint folk festival which are sectarian and tribal. There are, are there not, secret signs, symbols, special colours and shapes, great drums beaten to hypnotic rhythms, beaten I believe until the wrists of the performers bleed? There has been, I am told, an increase in what are popularly termed 'Kick the Pope' bands who specialise in wild and demotic songs of hate. These bands are preceded, are they not, by energetic and skilful young men who dance and caper and toss sticks and maces high in the air, catch them as they walk and twirl them round their bodies with incredible dexterity? These manifestations are not so unlike the gyrations of the negroes described in Mr Vachel Lindsay's poem as to make my humorously intended comparison totally invalid, Creaney?

CREANEY   They are expressions of loyalty, sir.

DEAN   Now, Creaney, do not attempt to argue with me that a parade of 'Kick the Pope' bands is a civilised way of expressing one's loyalty to the Queen and Commonwealth in the latter half of the twentieth century. Creaney? Come now, it is not unreasonable to describe these things as tribal?

CREANEY   If you say so, sir.

DEAN   I do say so, what do you say?

CREANEY   I say they are a reaction to the murdering bastards in the IRA, sir.

            (Pause. The CLASS look at each other, perhaps whistle or laugh nervously.)

DEAN   Creaney, the mathematics department tell me you are one of the brightest boys in this school. Do you know that?

CREANEY   So I've been told, sir.

DEAN   Well look Creaney, old chap, if you wish to fulfil your potential, you had better learn to moderate your language or no one will be even prepared to listen to your opinions.

CREANEY   They *are* murderers, sir.

DEAN   Yes indeed Creaney, but I hazard a guess that the majority of their parents were in fact

	married. Don't you think so, Creaney? Don't you think so?
CREANEY	I suppose so, sir.
DEAN	Well, don't be sullen and bitter about it, boy. You see, Creaney, if we are to make progress on this planet of ours it is sometimes better to forgive and forget; there is wrong on both sides, Creaney. You all have to live on this island after all. Someday soon you may have to live on it without the benefit of a referee, a referee who, I may add, is paying most of the bills and being shot at by both sides for his pains. Isn't he, Creaney?
CREANEY	I suppose so, sir.
DEAN	No good marching up and down like a lot of...like a lot of...marching up and...
	(*He goes into stare.*)
FIRST BOY	He's in a stare.
SECOND BOY	The Dean's in a stare.
THIRD BOY	Get the watch on him.
CLASS	(*chanting*) The Dean's in a stare, the Dean's in a stare, the Dean's in a stare.
CREANEY	Shhhhhhhhhhhhhhhhhhhh.
SECOND BOY	He's in a stare, Creaney.
CLASS	The Dean's in a stare. The Dean's in a stare...
	(*The danger of this speech and* CREANEY'*s daring should be emphasised. Perhaps other boys try to pull him to safety. He shoves them off. Gradually, they unite behind him.*)
CREANEY	Shut up! (*Pause.* CREANEY *approaches the* DEAN.) He looks like a crab. Like a dead crab. A boiled crab. (*Pause.*) You think the Orangemen are a bunch of niggers, Crab? Well that makes me a nigger. I bet that would surprise you Crab, this being a public school for the sons of gentlemen with a Royal Charter and all that.

Well, I'm the Orangeman in the venerable
woodpile, Crab, and my da, sorry father,
walks every Twelfth and his stockman Davy
Watson beside him and I walk behind the both
of them. The pavements of our village are
painted red white and blue for the occasion.
Probably a bit vulgar for your taste, Crab, but
an expression of loyalty to her Majesty the
Queen in the latter half of the twentieth
century. The Orange arch in our village is paid
for by my father out of his own pocket and it
says on it 'Love the brethren, Fear God,
Honour The King'. You English taught us that
Crab. The picture on the Lodge's banner is
one of Queen Victoria handing the Bible to a
bunch of grateful and respectful niggers. Do
you know what it says on that banner, Crab?
'The Secret of England's Greatness.' The
Bible. Remember it, Crab? The good book.
Black leather binding and thin fliffy pages
edged in gold? The King James version? The
Protestant Bible? You gave us that too, Crab,
and you want us to forget it just like that
parcel of wankers you call bishops in the
Church of England have forgotten it and threw
it...sorry thrown...have thrown it out. Oh, you
would like us to forget other things too. You
want us to be one big Irish family as happy as
pigs in shit, don't you? Forgive and forget,
isn't that it, Crab? Do you think *they* have
forgotten anything? Do you, Crab? Well, I
know they haven't because we haven't and we
won't and they won't. You see, Crab, you
English forget more easily than we do. You
shed your blood abroad. 'There's some corner
of a foreign field that is forever England.' Well
it's not like that here. Every drop is counted
here. Every corpse at the end of every lane is
numbered. The lanes are counted too. Every
stone is like a body. Each gate, gap, ditch.
Each field, each sod. Every widow's
tear. All counted; all to be accounted for. So

fuck off Englishman if that's what you really
want to do. Make your feeble excuses and go.
Tell everybody how hard you tried, that we
were impossible and that you did your best and
go home for your toast and tea and leave us to
stronger meat.

(*The* CLASS *shout obscenities at the* DEAN. *The bell
goes, they stop shouting and remain rigid as the* DEAN
comes out of his stare and leaves. CREANEY *begins a
chant and the* CLASS *joins in.*)

CLASS   There's a pub, there's a pub on the Lambeg
Road.
Biddy McDowell Biddy McDowell
Biddy McDowell Dowell Dowell.
There's a pub, there's a pub on the Lambeg
Road.
Biddy McDowell Biddy McDowell
Biddy McDowell Dowell Dowell.
There's a pub, there's a pub on the Lambeg
Road.
Biddy McDowell Biddy McDowell
Biddy McDowell Dowell Dowell.
I'll give you thirty shillings for your one pound
ten.

With your one pound ten (*They wheel off the
desks.*)
With your one pound ten!
I'll give you thirty shillings for your one pound
ten.
January February March
No!
April May June?
No!
July?
(*A tremendous yell, off.*)
AYE!

(*As the class exits,* BARRY *and* CREANEY *take off
their coats and throw them on the ground. The scene
changes as if they were outside. Birds sing,
grasshoppers click, the sun shines brightly. In the
distance is the sound of a cricket match, ripples of*

applause etc. BARRY *and* CREANEY *lie close together.*
CREANEY *is now shirtless, sunbathing.*)

CREANEY   It's hot, Dum Dum.

BARRY   Yes.

CREANEY   Bloody hot.

BARRY   Yes.

CREANEY   Well, take your shirt off.

BARRY   OK. (*He does so.*)

CREANEY   Listen to the grasshoppers.

BARRY   Yes.

CREANEY   Rubbing their little legs together.

BARRY   Big actually. For an insect. Huge in fact.
            (*Pause.*)

CREANEY   Very fricative.

BARRY   Yes.

CREANEY   Frico, fricare, to rub.

BARRY   Yes.

CREANEY   Sexy beggars.

BARRY   Grasshoppers?

CREANEY   Lie back, Dum Dum.

BARRY   Why?

CREANEY   You'll not get a tan like that.

BARRY   Who says I want a tan?

CREANEY   The girls like a tan. They go for skin. This
            phantom woman in the garden will like a tan;
            like you all coppery.

            (BARRY *lies back besides* CREANEY.)

            You've got a hair on your chest, Dum Dum.
            One hair. No, here's another. Don't move,
            I'm looking for more. (*Pause.*)

BARRY   Did you mean all that stuff you said to the
            Dean?

CREANEY   Yes. Look at this! A mini forest on Dum
            Dum's chest.

BARRY   I didn't agree.

CREANEY   Who don't you agree with, Dum Dum? No
                 more, no more, the rest is as smooth as a
                 baby's bum. Who didn't…With whom did you
                 not agree, Dum Dum?

BARRY   You.

                 (*Pause.*)

CREANEY   Why?

BARRY   They are not all in the IRA any more than we
                 are in the UVF.

CREANEY   They all want a united Ireland.

BARRY   They don't all want it violently, mostly they
                 want it peacefully, with agreement.

CREANEY   They still want it.

BARRY   Well, let's have an agreement between all those
                 who reject violence.

CREANEY   Listen Dum Dum, whatever agreement our
                 politicians make with their politicians it is
                 necessary for their politicians to tell them that
                 this agreement that they have just signed with
                 our politicians is a democratic and peaceful
                 step to a united Ireland and it is necessary for
                 our politicians to tell us that this same
                 agreement is the greatest defence of the union
                 since The Clyde Valley ran the guns into
                 Larne. And we being the awkward parcel of
                 cunts that we are believe their politicians and
                 they being not a lot different believe ours so
                 everyone manages to be betrayed by the same
                 agreement and the politicians who made it are
                 redundant and a new lot have taken over by
                 promising not to sell out the people like the last
                 shower. (*Pause.*) It's never going to get any
                 better, Dum Dum. Not really better, not till
                 someone gives in. We're not. They're not. So.
                 (*He is tickling* BARRY's *chest with a piece of grass.*)

BARRY   That tickles.

CREANEY   I'm marking out new areas for aforestation.

               (*Sings softly to the tune of 'Galway Bay.'*)

               'Oh if there's going to be a fight hereafter
               And I'm sure there's going to be,
               We'll make the Fenian blood flow like holy
                   water
               Down the Belfast lough into the Irish sea.'

               (*Pause.*)

BARRY   I'm definitely going to kiss that girl next
               Wednesday, the one next door. I'll be home
               just before lunch and I bet she's in the garden.
               Bound to be in this weather, isn't she?

CREANEY   Oh yes.

               (*Pause.*)

BARRY   Do you really think there's going to be a fight?

CREANEY   Yes. (*Pause. Sings softly.*) 'Lero Lero Lillibulero
               Lero Lero Bullen-a-la!'

BARRY   What's that?

CREANEY   'Lillibulero?' Protestant marching song from
               sixteen eighty-nine, 'Lillibulero bullen-a-la.'

               (*Burst of applause in the distance.*)

BARRY   What's that?

CREANEY   Somebody's out.

BARRY   Will I go and see?

CREANEY   Do you want to?

BARRY   No.

               (*Pause.* CREANEY *very close, almost on top of him,
               tickling his face with a piece of grass.*)

               I don't think our side have the nerve for it.

CREANEY   What?

BARRY   A fight. I don't think they have the bottle.

CREANEY   Shit.

BARRY	I don't think they believe in the place enough.
CREANEY	(*horrified*) Ach, Dum Dum.
BARRY	It's always seemed to me that the country isn't really ours.
CREANEY	(*total disbelief*) What?
BARRY	The tradition and the history are all theirs. The Gaelic language, the music, the dancing, all that sort of thing. We dispossessed them. Discrimination.
CREANEY	What discrimination?
BARRY	Ach come off it, you're not going to say it didn't happen?
CREANEY	Well...
BARRY	Save that crap for the Dean but don't give it to me.
CREANEY	Well, it wasn't as bad as all that.
BARRY	Bad enough...(*Stopping his reply.*) I mean it was bad enough to give them a cause. We always seem to be in the wrong, hanging on by our fingernails, surrounded. I've always felt we were in the wrong, about everything, except that I don't think we deserve to be murdered, but in the wrong.
CREANEY	Listen Dum Dum, that's not true.
BARRY	It's as if they had first claim. They are the descendants of the ancient Gaelic past. They put up the street names in Irish as a sort of reproach. You may have built these hovels to stick us in but we were here long ago, and anyway ya boo suck you can't read this Balatha something or other. It's as if they are the people and we are the interlopers, colonisers; we have no history in this place and when it comes to a real fight we'll just get up and go.

CREANEY   Listen, Dum Dum. There's a lake not far from
                   where I live. Four bronze trumpets were found
                   in that lake; they're in the museum. I've been
                   to see them. Everybody assumes that anything
                   like that is Gaelic, everybody assumes that
                   anything really old is Gaelic. But these things
                   were made before the Gaels came to Ireland.
                   They were made by a different people, a
                   people driven out of Ulster by Gaels invading
                   from the south. The Gaels won it from them
                   by the sword and drove them into Scotland.
                   But they came back, back to their own, like the
                   Jews to the Holy Land. They are us, we are
                   they; our people. And we didn't come back
                   yesterday like the Jews. We came back four
                   hundred years ago. Won it back. With sword.
                   We worked the land, like the Jews, made the
                   desert bloom. My county is called the orchard
                   county. It blossoms. (*They lie close together and*
                   CREANEY *speaks quietly, seductively.*) There's a
                   fort near that lake, that's where these people
                   had their kings and their religion. Nobody now
                   knows the meaning of it all. (CREANEY *pulls his*
                   coat across BARRY*'s lower abdomen. Beneath it, his*
                   hand starts a gentle rhythmic movement.) Away to
                   the south they built a line of ditches where the
                   border now is to keep out the rest of Ireland.
                   It's called the Black Pigs dyke. It's just bumps
                   in the ground now. But it's there. (*A distant*
                   shout of howzat, clapping.)

BARRY   (*very quietly*) Someone else is out.

CREANEY   (*very softly.*) I don't care if the whole fucking
                   team is out, Dum Dum. I don't want to know.
                   Don't move. Just lie still, very still. That's it.
                   It's alright, just lie still, still, still...

                   (*Long pause. The sound of the grasshoppers becomes*
                   oppressively loud. A distant sound of the clunk of a
                   ball on a bat; ripples of applause.)

                   OK? (*Pause.*) OK, Dum?

BARRY	Yes.
	(*Pause.*)
CREANEY	Nothing like the narles, of course. Doesn't come near it. When you get the narles, you sort of explode. Your senses take over and you experience refinements of feeling that you could never have imagined even in your rarest fantasies.
BARRY	How do you know?
CREANEY	Everybody knows that, Dum Dum. Hey, Dum Dum?
BARRY	What?
CREANEY	What about me?
	(BARRY *runs off. The* CLASS *enters, bringing on furniture for the* DEAN's *study.* CREANEY *exits in the opposite direction to* BARRY.)
DUNBAR	(*trying to give money to* BUTLER.) Ah, come on Butler, come on.
BUTLER	No.
DUNBAR	We've all chipped in, for Christ's sake.
McKENNA	Be a sport.
RICHARDS	Come on, Butler.
BUTLER	No. No. No.
DUNBAR	Typical bloody day boy.
RICHARDS	Get's you all excited and then cops out.
McKENNA	Cop out.
DUNBAR	Bloody cop out.
BUTLER	All right! If Bobby comes.
McKENNA	Bobby?
LOWRY	I'll go if Roy does.
BUTLER	What do you want?
RICHARDS	What do they have?

DUNBAR	What do they have, Butler?
BUTLER	I don't know.
DUNBAR	There was enough bloody oul yap out of you about it.
BUTLER	I said I saw it, all I said was I saw it.
LOWRY	Just saw it.
DUNBAR	All talk.
ALL	Talk. Talk. Talk.
BUTLER	I was on the top deck of a bus, for Christ's sake. I can't friggin' fly, can I?
LOWRY	Can't fly at all.

(PATTERSON *enters.*)

DUNBAR	What do they have in sex shops, Patterson?
PATTERSON	Judy dolls, dildoes, vibrators, Grow-It-Big pills, aphrodisiacs, West German porno playing cards.
RICHARDS	Jesus.
DUNBAR	What'll we get, boys?
RICHARDS	A selection.

(*They exit. Lights come up on the* DEAN*'s study.* BARRY *stands in front of him.*)

DEAN	Naturally I have no wish to dwell on this aspect but the position is not without its personal risks, is it?
BARRY	No, sir.
DEAN	Well I admire your father, Dunham. I remember him as a boy at this school. He had a fine analytical mind. He was, as you know, head of house and head of the school. Ulster needs more men like him, men of principle, men who are prepared to uphold the rule of

law however difficult. They stand between us and anarchy, Dunham. Your father has my congratulations and admiration. Tell him so, please.

BARRY   Yes, sir.

DEAN   Your exeat. (*He hands him a piece of paper.*)

BARRY   Thank you, sir.

DEAN   I like the changes you made in the poem.

BARRY   Oh...thank you.

DEAN   'I reject despair and the wish to turn
            From the pre-ordained design.
            Through hate and fear the homelands burn,
            Fate and future I will not resign.'
            That has a brave ring, a positive ring, good.
            Good. Now. There's always a now, isn't there,
            or a but eh?....Now one more stanza to say
            that you must build on the good traditions in
            the Ulster community. Well?

BARRY   Yes, sir.

DEAN   Think about it on your exeat.

BARRY   Yes, sir.

            (*Pause.*)

DEAN   Is there anything else?

BARRY   Yes, sir.

DEAN   Well, tell me.

BARRY   I was wondering, sir...Well, I was wondering
            what...the possibility...

DEAN   Speak Dunham. Speak in sentences.

BARRY   What are the possibilities of becoming a day
            boy, sir?

DEAN   A *day boy?*

BARRY   Yes, sir.

DEAN	Whatever for?
BARRY	I was just wondering, sir.
DEAN	Well stop wondering Dunham, and explain. Give me reasons.
	(*Pause.*)
BARRY	It's just a feeling, sir.
DEAN	Hardly an explanation, is it?
BARRY	No, sir.
DEAN	We cannot take decisions on the strength of our feelings alone, can we, Dunham?
BARRY	No, sir.
DEAN	Where would your father be if he had to decide cases on how he felt at the time?
BARRY	I don't know, sir.
DEAN	Are you unhappy?
BARRY	Yes, sir.
DEAN	Why are you unhappy?
BARRY	I'm not sure, sir.
DEAN	Dunham, old chap, we are going round in circles, aren't we?
BARRY	Yes, sir.
DEAN	Have you spoken to your father about this?
BARRY	No, sir.
DEAN	Well, I suggest you do Dunham, when you go home. I had thought of you as one of my prefects next year; I had even thought of you following in your father's footsteps and becoming head of house, head of school maybe, who knows? It should also be said that the headmaster has set his face against any further decline in the numbers of the boarding department so your reasons would have to be

good ones. Look, old chap, you go home, talk
it over with your parents and I will listen
seriously to anything you have to say. Can I be
fairer than that?

BARRY   No, sir.

(*The* CLASS *enters to move the* DEAN's *furniture.*
BARRY *and the* DEAN *exit.*)

BUTLER   There was an Elder out of our church on the
picket, for Christ's sake!

BOY   Excuses, excuses.

BUTLER   They were singing hymns!

LOWRY   Hymns.

DUNBAR   You're yellow, Butler.

BUTLER   Handing out tracts.

LOWRY   Tracts.

BUTLER   Bobby ran away.

LOWRY   I was f...f...f...f...

BUTLER   And he had the money.

DUNBAR   The pair of you bolloxed it.

LOWRY   I was frightened my mummy might f...f...f...

WOMBAT   Bollocks!

BUTLER   You try! You try!

DUNBAR   We will. We will.

LOWRY   F...find out.

(*They exit with the furniture.* BARRY *crosses the stage
quickly.* CREANEY *enters. It is the first time they have
seen each other since the cricket match.*)

CREANEY   Where are you heading for, Dum Dum?

BARRY   Exeat.

CREANEY   To paradise!

(BARRY *laughs.*)

Maybe she'll do more than kiss you.

(BARRY *laughs again.*)

CREANEY   A bit of the old F3, eh? The aesthetically
            beauooootifullll breasts; just ease up the old
            Youth for Christ T shirt and wowwwwwwww!

(BARRY *chuckles in complicity.*)

CREANEY   Is she the religious type?

BARRY   I don't know.

CREANEY   They can be the hottest little ravers you know.

BARRY   Can they?

CREANEY   God yes, especially after a gospel meeting.
            When they have been washed in the blood of
            the lamb...Jeeeesssuuuuuuuss!

(BARRY *laughs. He is hooked on* CREANEY*'s
fantasy.*)

CREANEY   Wish it was me.

BARRY   (*delighted with himself*) God.

CREANEY   Lucky bugger.

BARRY   (*feeling like a lucky bugger*) I'll give her one for
            you.

CREANEY   You do that.

BARRY   Should I ask her? You know, when...when
            we're together...in the garden....

CREANEY   In the garden of delights.

BARRY   In *the garden of delights*. Should I ask her to
            kiss?...or...

CREANEY   Jesus no. Just do it. They expect it.

BARRY   Do they?

CREANEY   Jesus yes.

BARRY   I see.

CREANEY   Listen, Dum Dum, while you're making up
              your mind deciding whether to or not they're
              standing there saying to themselves, what the
              hell's keeping him?

BARRY   Honestly?

CREANEY   They're probably thinking, 'Is he queer or
              have his balls not dropped?'

BARRY   They don't talk like that.

CREANEY   Oh God yes, they're far filthier than us.

BARRY   Are they?

CREANEY   You can't take them by surprise either, they
              have a sort of inbuilt radar they always know
              you're looking at them. They're naturally vain
              you see, so all you've got to do is send signals,
              body language, and you'll get the old come-on.
              Kissing's nothing, Dum Dum. Kissing's easy.

BARRY   (*laughing*) Easy.

CREANEY   (*chanting, football style*) Easy, easy, easy.

BARRY   (*delighted by the prospects*) Easy, easy, easy.

CREANEY   Body language!

BARRY   Easy, easy, easy...

CREANEY   Signals!

BARRY   Easy, easy, easy...

CREANEY   *Lucky bugger!*

BARRY   Easy, easy, easy...

              (*As* BARRY *chants, the fence comes on and when he
              turns, he is suddenly faced with it.* ANGELA *is once
              more playing swing ball.*)

ANGELA   One hundred and nine, one hundred and ten,
              etc.

              (BARRY *moves closer. The fence separates them.*
              ANGELA *continues to play and counts out loud.*
              BARRY *is hoping that she will notice him but she
              merely continues to concentrate on her game. He moves
              about to catch her line of sight but does not*

succeed. He tries a wave of the hand. She takes no notice. He waves both hands. Still no reaction. He jumps up and down, gesticulating wildly, clowning ridiculously and getting quite out of control. Finally ANGELA *notices him and stops to stare at his antics. Clearly, she thinks he is mad.* BARRY *eventually notices that she is staring at him and he is overcome wth embarrassment. They stand looking at each other across the fence in silence. She backs away a step or two, obviously suspicious.*)

BARRY   (*strangulated*) Ahhhh...

     (ANGELA *moves back a couple of steps.*)

MARION   (*calling off*) Barry!

BARRY   (*tentatively to* ANGELA) Hello.

MARION   (*calling off, louder*) Barry!

BARRY   I was...I was just...I didn't know...at least...

     (ANGELA *shakes her head and walks away.*)

MARION   (*off*) *Barry!*

BARRY   (*turning to shout to his mother, off*) *Wait!* (*He turns back but* ANGELA *has gone.*)

MARION   (*still calling, off*) Barry! Come in and get changed at once!

     (BARRY *looks desperately back towards the direction of his mother's call, and then steps forward to the fence, straining to see* ANGELA.)

     (*off*) Barrrrreeeeeee!

     (BARRY *half turns.*)

     (*BLACK OUT*)

INTERVAL

ACT TWO

MARION *Dunham is in her bedrooom changing. Clothes and accessories are laid out on the double bed. She examines herself critically in front of a mirror and calls through to* BARRY, *offstage.*

MARION	There's a new tie on the back of the chair.
BARRY	(*sullen, defensive, examining it critically*) Yes.
MARION	Daddy chose it.
BARRY	(*resigned*) Yes.
MARION	Thank him, won't you? (*She is dissatisfied with the dress. She searches to find that little extra that will set it off, transform her appearance.*)
BARRY	(*at the door of her room, taking her by surprise*) Why is there a police car in the road?
MARION	It's the guard; your father has to be guarded, Barry.
BARRY	He's not here.
MARION	The house has to be guarded; we have to be guarded. You know that, Barry dear. We had a visit from the security branch. Such a nice man.
BARRY	Why did he accept?
MARION	Accept what dear?
BARRY	The judgeship.
MARION	Accept the judgeship?
BARRY	That's what I asked.
MARION	Because...isn't that obvious?
BARRY	No.
MARION	I thought you would have been proud.
BARRY	Who said I wasn't?
MARION	Nobody but...
BARRY	I am proud.

MARION   Are you?

BARRY   I said I was!

     (*Pause.*)

MARION   It's a great honour. He feels it's his duty. We should all do our duty. Shouldn't we?

BARRY   Yes.

MARION   It isn't right, is it?

BARRY   What?

MARION   The dress.

BARRY   Oh.

MARION   Oh God, he'll hate it, I know he'll hate it. Unzip me Barry, love, and I'll do a quick change. (BARRY *unzips her dress.*) Oh my God, we are going to be late. (*She dives among her dresses, selecting, rejecting, re-selecting, re-rejecting.*)

BARRY   Did he ask you?

MARION   (*distracted*) What?

BARRY   (*relentless*) Did he ask you if you wanted him to be a judge?

MARION   Well of course he did dear...do you think this one will be alright? I only wore it once, at the Chief Constable's Christmas party. I'm nearly sure he liked it...

BARRY   What did you say?

MARION   (*concentrating on her dress*) What did I say to what?

BARRY   What did you say when he asked you what you thought of him becoming a judge?

MARION   What did I say?

BARRY   Yes.

MARION   (*trying on a dress*) I said, I said...I said yes, of course.

BARRY   No, you didn't.

MARION	What?
BARRY	I said you didn't say yes.
MARION	Barry don't be silly.
BARRY	When I asked you what you said, you hesitated.
MARION	Nonsense.
BARRY	You hesitated twice.
MARION	Barry, we haven't time for this.
BARRY	Don't avoid the issue.
MARION	What issue?
BARRY	Twice you hesitated and then said 'yes of course', in that special way you have.
MARION	What special way?
BARRY	The way that means, 'that's what I would have said, should have said, ought to have said, was expected to say, if I had ever been asked, that is'.
MARION	(*puzzled, nervous*) Barry?
BARRY	I remember when I was eight and was being sent away to boarding school people used to ask you if I was looking forward to it, and you said 'Oh yes, of course he is,' just like you did now.
MARION	Barry?
BARRY	*And* you hadn't even asked me, so you didn't know; how the hell could you know? You'd never asked me!
MARION	(*alarmed now*) Barry?
BARRY	I was dreading it. Did you know that? I was shit scared!
MARION	BARRY!
BARRY	Sorry.

MARION	Why are you asking all this now?
BARRY	What difference does the time make, the time is irrelevant.
	(*Pause.*)
MARION	Barry? (*She approaches him tenderly but he steps back abruptly.*) Don't move away, son. (*Pause.*) Barry, what is it, love?
BARRY	Can I become a day boy?
MARION	A day boy?
BARRY	Mummy, you heard. A day boy. I want to be a day boy. You know — a boy who goes to school in the morning and comes home in the evening. I want to stop boarding.
MARION	Why?
BARRY	Just.
MARION	There must be reasons, Barry.
BARRY	There are lots.
MARION	But what? You accused me of not listening or not asking...What reasons?
BARRY	Girls.
MARION	What?
BARRY	(*losing his temper*) Oh for Christ's sake, Mummy, stop saying what! I said girls. G.I.R.L.S. You know, with skirts on. You were one. Once. There are no girls at school.
MARION	But it's boys' school.
BARRY	Oh Mummy do you have to be bloody thick as well as just silly?
MARION	Barry!
BARRY	Sorry. Sorry I didn't mean that. Sorry.
MARION	I should think so too.

BARRY	For Christ's sake, Mummy, I said I was sorry. You repeat everything I say, when I ask you a question you ask it all over again.
MARION	Do I?
BARRY	You're doing it again, you've got so used to not being asked questions, real questions, you don't know how to answer them!
MARION	That's not true.
BARRY	Of course it's true.
MARION	Barry, what's got into you?
BARRY	I want to be a day boy!
	(*Pause.*)
MARION	Well you'll have to ask your father.
BARRY	You decide.
MARION	Decide?
BARRY	Oh Mummy, for God's sake stop it!
MARION	(*shouting back at him*) I can't decide!
BARRY	Why not? Why not? You're half the marriage, aren't you?
MARION	Barry...
BARRY	Or are you?
MARION	Barry!
BARRY	What do you decide?
MARION	Barry, this is not fair!
BARRY	What?
MARION	You are afraid to ask your father and so...
BARRY	What?
MARION	...so you pick a quarrel with me!...
BARRY	What?
MARION	...as if it's my fault!

BARRY   What do you decide, Mummy?

             (*Pause.*)

MARION   Lots of things. We decide things together.
             Marriage is a partnership. He's a lot older
             than I am and...well, he's always decided that
             sort of thing, I decide other...I'm not a cipher,
             Barry. I'm not. (*Pause. He looks at her.*) I'm not.

BARRY   Will you ask him if I can become a day boy?

MARION   Yes.

BARRY   Today?

MARION   But he's being made a judge today.

BARRY   I know, I know, I know!

             (*Pause. They are face to face again.*)

MARION   Barry love, we're going to be late. I don't
             know what your father will say when we...

BARRY   I know what he'll say.

MARION   What?

BARRY   (*imitating*) 'Marion, Marion, how do you
             manage it?'

MARION   Oh God he will he will...(*She frantically gets
             ready.*) *Black out. The lights come up on* BILL's
             robing room where he is robing. He turns towards
             MARION *and* BARRY *as they enter.*)

BILL   Hello Barry. (*To Marion*) How do you manage
             it, Marion? Every time. In God's name, how
             do you do it?

MARION   Sorry Bill I...

BILL   Do you realise that you have missed a chance
             to have a sherry with the Lord Chancellor?

MARION   Who?

BILL   The Lord Chancellor. He came over himself.

MARION   Oh I didn't know.

BILL   How could you have known, Marion? Even I
             didn't know. However I was on time.

MARION	I'm sorry, Bill.
BILL	Well there'll be another opportunity later.
MARION	Oh good.
BILL	He is showing solidarity with the legal system here in Northern Ireland and with Rory, of course.
MARION	Yes.
BILL	This was Rory's room.
MARION	Oh...I didn't know.
BARRY	How could you have, Mummy?
MARION	I said I didn't.
BILL	Rory O'Callaghan and I were at university together, called to the bar together and took silk together. And now...I am robing in his room. Actually some of his books are still on the shelf over there.
MARION	Oh.
BILL	Perhaps you would like to take them to Imelda sometime?
MARION	Yes...of course...poor Imelda.
BILL	She's being very brave.
MARION	Yes.
BILL	These neck bands have a bar in the middle of each to show that I'm in mourning.
MARION	Look, Barry.
BARRY	I'm looking, Mummy.
MARION	(*mouthing at him*) In mourning for Rory O'Callaghan.
BARRY	I heard!
BILL	Each of the judge's robes has a particular historical significance.
BARRY	Can I become a day boy?
	(*Pause*)
MARION	Barry!
BARRY	You said to ask.

MARION	Not now dear...
BARRY	*You* weren't going to ask *now*.
MARION	(*whimpered entreaty*) Barry!
BARRY	Can I become a day boy?
BILL	Barry, I think we should discuss this later.
BARRY	What's wrong with now?
BILL	If you can't see that, I have grave doubts about your intelligence...
BARRY	I want to stop being a bord...
BILL	*As* for your insensitivity...it amazes me. I wouldn't have thought it of you. (*Pause.*)
MARION	Perhaps you should listen to him, Bill.
BILL	*Of course I will listen to him!*
MARION	Of course.
BILL	At the right time and in the right place. (*Pause.*)
MARION	(*mouthing to* BARRY) Apologise. Barry?
BARRY	Sorry. I only asked...Sorry.
BILL	Are you?
BARRY	I said I was sorry.
BILL	Prompted by your mother.
BARRY	Yes but...
MARION	He said he was sorry, Bill.
BILL	Very well...He said he's sorry...good. (*Pause as* BILL *takes his gown and continues as before.*)
BILL	*Each* of the judge's robes has a particular historical significance.
MARION	(*pointing to gown and mouthing to* BARRY) Ask him about...
BARRY	(*mouthing back*) What?
MARION	(*same*) The gown.
BARRY	What is the thing you are putting on now, Daddy?

BILL	A gown.
BARRY	(*his mother prompting*) What's if for?
BILL	The gown is of ecclesiastical origin.
MARION	Ecclesiastical, Barry.
BARRY	I heard.
BILL	Each of the judges' robes has a particular historical significance.
MARION	(*to* BARRY) A particular hist...
BILL	And of course they enhance the dignity and the solemnity of the judicial process.
BARRY	I see.
BILL	It's interesting to note that the Americans abolished all the trappings of state in the Nascent republic but the one that came back was the wearing of judicial robes. You see the world is grateful for at least one thing we gave them, no matter what some Irishmen think. Isn't that so, Barry? Isn't that so?
BARRY	Yes.
BILL	Now look, young man, I will allow you to put your case, you know. But I warn you it had better be a pretty good case. I don't want the first litigant in my court found guilty of wasting my time. Do I?
BARRY	No.
BILL	Now this is an interesting hood, called a casting hood or sometimes known as the gun case hood or gun case.
MARION	Is it for trying cases with guns in them?
BILL	(*laughing*) Oh Marion, Marion.
BARRY	(*mortified*) Oh Mummy, don't be stupid.
MARION	I'm not stupid!
BILL	Silly would be a kinder word, Barry.

BARRY	Sorry Mummy, silly.
MARION	I'm not silly either!
BILL	Of course you're not, my dear. It is called a gun case hood because being narrower at one end it bore a fancied resemblance to a canvas case for a sporting gun.
MARION	I never thought of that.
BARRY	How could you have thought of it?
MARION	I said I didn't.
BILL	The gun case must be placed over and not under the stole, why is that Barry?
BARRY	I don't know.
BILL	I did not expect you to know, I expected you to ask.
BARRY	Why do you wear the gun case over the stole?
BILL	Wearing the hood on the right side of the tippet signifies the judge's temporal dignity.
MARION	Temporal?
BARRY	Worldly as opposed to spiritual.
BILL	Good boy, Barry, good boy.
BARRY	The lords temporal and spiritual, that's bishops, Mummy.
MARION	I did know.
BILL	Marion, a change of plan for this afternoon. We've been invited to a small reception for the Lord Chancellor before he flies back to London.
MARION	Oh Bill, will I need to change?
BILL	No I...why didn't you wear your new dress?
MARION	I tried it on but...
BILL	I had thought, something new, for the occasion.

BARRY	Oh thank you for the tie.
BILL	(*preparing to leave*) I'll let you into a secret, young man, your mother bought it. By the way, you are invited too.
BARRY	But...
MARION	Oh Barry!
BILL	I'll ask the tipstaff to knock and he'll show you where to go.
MARION	Just think of that, Barry!
BILL	(*leaving*) Thank you both for coming. I am proud to have you both here with me, it makes the awesome responsibility bearable, to know you are there. (*Exits.*)
MARION	The Lord Chancellor? Oh Barry!
BARRY	I have to go home!
MARION	Why!
BARRY	I have to that's all. I don't want to go to a bloody reception! He never thinks of anybody else!
MARION	Barry, what a dreadful thing to say! Your father is being made a judge, the Lord Chancellor of England is here!
BARRY	I know.
MARION	Your father agreed to become a judge because his friend Rory O'Callaghan was shot dead by the IRA.
BARRY	(*nasty coals of fire*) I know, I know.
MARION	(*heaping them on*) Your daddy always said it was so brave of Rory, a Roman Catholic, to become a judge and when he was asked to sit in Rory's place he felt he couldn't refuse.
BARRY	(*furious at the ungenerous position in which he finds himself*) Mummy, surely you know that I know all that?

MARION	Well, if you do dear, why don't you show some respect?
BARRY	I do, Mummy, I do! I do respect him, admire him. I am proud of him...I don't love him.
MARION	(*horrified*) Barry?
BARRY	I can't.
MARION	Barry!
BARRY	(*sobbing*) I can't, I can't, I can't.
MARION	(*as knocking is heard*) Barry love, Barry love, Barry...

(*They exit. The* CLASS *enters.* DUNBAR, BUTLER *and* LOWRY *enter with cricket gear.* LOWRY *clumsily carries his bag and bat. The others remove the furniture.*)

DUNBAR	Come on, Bobby.
BUTLER	Robinson says they're monsters.
DUNBAR	Who have you picked anyway?

(BOBBY *drops his cricket gear.*)

BUTLER	Watch the bat, Bobby.
DUNBAR	(*consulting his list*) Hamilton, you, me, McKenna?
BUTLER	Why not?
DUNBAR	We can't have McKenna.
BUTLER	He's bloody good.
DUNBAR	We can't have McKenna.
BUTLER	This is a non-sectarian cricket team, Dunbar.
DUNBAR	That doesn't mean I have to play on the same side as that Fenian fucker!
BUTLER	Who would you have instead, then? (*He looks at* BOBBY.)

BOBBY	Me! I'll play.
DUNBAR	Ay, well anyway. You keep score, Bobby. You're really good at that.

(They exit. PATTERSON enters with CREANEY.)

PATTERSON	But you implied plenty. The faithful Dunners had a day at home you said. You hinted at the possibilities in a garden, a garden of delights. Come on, Creaney, don't be a tease and tell me what Dunham was up to in the garden of the forbidden fruit.
CREANEY	He was going to kiss a girl.
PATTERSON	Is that all? Hardly the tree of the knowledge of good and evil that.
CREANEY	He hasn't done if before.
PATTERSON	Not kissed a girl?
CREANEY	Not properly.
PATTERSON	At his age?

(BARRY enters.)

	Hello Dunners. Well?
BARRY	Well what?
PATTERSON	How did it go?
BARRY	Oh great.
PATTERSON	Tell us all about it, man. We are agog. Aren't we agog, Creaney?
BARRY	I met the Lord Chancellor of England.
PATTERSON	In the garden?
BARRY	At a reception.
PATTERSON	But what happened in the garden?
BARRY	What garden?
PATTERSON	The girl in the garden. The one you were going to kiss for the first time. You can tell us. Well?

BARRY	Fuck you, Creaney! (*He walks out.*)
PATTERSON	My goodness. He is uptight. He is very uptight. Poor old Dunners. Did I tell you, Creaney, that I intend to become a psychiatrist?
CREANEY	*Shut up!*
PATTERSON	No need to lose the bap.
CREANEY	(*going*) Mind your own bloody business!
PATTERSON	(*shouting after him.*) You made it my business, you know! You told me. (*Pause.*) I suppose the most difficult part of psychiatry is actually getting the patient to stay still long enough to listen to one's words of wisdom and understanding.
	(*Other members of the* CLASS *cross the stage throwing a cricket ball about and* PATTERSON *sees them. They also bring on a props basket and chair.*)
	Hey Brown, Lowry, McKenna, wait till you hear this.
	(*they gather together*) Dunham went home on a exeat and he had it all arranged to meet this femme fatale in a garden and he chickened out. All laid on and he…makes you wonder, doesn't it. I mean he's never kissed a girl. Never.
1ST BOY	Never kissed one?
PATTERSON	Apparently not.
	(*A mounting conspiracy of amazement and laughter.*)
2ND BOY	Jesus!
3RD BOY	Never had a sodding kiss!
PATTERSON	Not one!
1ST BOY	Christ!
2ND BOY	Bloody hell!
LOWRY	(*a stutter*) F…f…
3RD BOY	I mean, for Christ's sake!

1st Boy	Hell's gates!
Lowry	F...fff...
2nd Boy	Kissing? Bloody kissing?
Lowry	F...f...f...f..:
3rd Boy	I mean, good God, bloody hell's bloody gates, bloody kissing?
Lowry	F...f...f...f...f...
1st Boy	Jesus fucking Christ kissing, fucking kissing?
Lowry	F...f...f...*fuck!*

(*Black out.* BARRY *is spotted high above the stage on a crossbeam above the school hall.* CREANEY *approaches cautiously.*)

CREANEY	Dum Dum? (*Pause.*) It's hard to see where you're going up here...(*He slides along the beam towards* BARRY.) Hey, Dum Dum, is this safe? (*Beside him.*) Jesus, it's not safe at all. (*Pause.*) What are you doing up here, Dum Dum?
BARRY	I often come here.
CREANEY	Why?
BARRY	To get away from everything.
	(*Pause.*)
CREANEY	Are you alright?
BARRY	Yes.
CREANEY	Oh no you're not.
BARRY	(*tense, shouting*) Yes I am!
	(*Pause.*)
CREANEY	I'm sorry, Dum Dum.
BARRY	What for?
CREANEY	Telling that creep Patterson.
BARRY	It doesn't matter.
CREANEY	Yes it does. I betrayed you.

BARRY	Everyone betrays everyone in this place.
CREANEY	I'm not everyone, at least I thought I wasn't. I hate traitors, Lundies; I'm no Lundy. Creaney means Cruthin. That's the name of the people who lived here before the Gaels. The ones I told you about. Remember? I hate Lundies, Dum Dum. I'm sorry.
BARRY	It's OK.
	(*Pause.*)
CREANEY	I didn't know this place existed.
BARRY	I found it last year when I was on the lighting team for *King Lear*. If you look down there you can see the whole school scurrying about, jostling, fighting, yittering yapping mouths, rules, bells, smells, bodies...up here I can breathe.
CREANEY	Kissing's nothing to worry about Dum Dum.
BARRY	So you said.
CREANEY	Doesn't signify, the narles is the only thing that signifies and I haven't had that either, worst luck.
BARRY	(*suddenly tightening, a muscular and verbal paroxysm causes him to wobble dangerously*) Damn, damn, DAMN!
CREANEY	(*alarmed*) Jesus take it easy, Dum Dum.
BARRY	Sometimes I have moments of self loathing so intense, I have such a physical hatred of myself that I could spew up at the thought of my own puerility!
CREANEY	Don't do it too hard, Dum Dum, or you'll fall full forty fucking feet to the fucking floor.
	(BARRY *laughs.*)
CREANEY	What's the joke?
BARRY	You are. Your alliteration.

CREANEY   I don't mind what it is Dum Dum just so long as you don't...

BARRY   ...fall full forty fucking feet to the fucking floor.

CREANEY   (*joining in*)...to the fucking floor.

               (*They both laugh.*)

BARRY   There was a fence in the way. A fence? I knew it was there, for God's sake. Then I had to go and watch my father being made a judge and be proud. And then instead of getting back to the garden in the afternoon we were invited to a reception and I had to go and talk to the Lord Chancellor of England.

CREANEY   What did that oul bollocks have to say for himself?

BARRY   'And what are the traditions of your school, young man?'

CREANEY   Wanking, that's what I'd have said.

BARRY   I gibbered the sort of thing Howlie comes out with on Founder's Day...

CREANEY   Wanking. Imaginative wanking, sir.

BARRY   And he said 'Do you realise young man?' They always call you young man, don't they? 'Do you realise young man, that your father and his colleagues on the bench stand between the preservation of those traditions and anarchy?' 'Yes, sir,' I said.

CREANEY   Oh old England can still rely on us, sir, wankers to the last man.

BARRY   (*imitating the Lord Chancellor*) 'Things fall apart, the centre cannot hold, mere anarchy is loosed upon the world.' 'What is that from young man?' He was so chuffed when I told him Yeats. I was the star of the afternoon. My father was delighted. Proud of me.

CREANEY   Why don't they tell the truth?

BARRY	Who?
CREANEY	All those old buffers who've done time in kips like this. They know what it's like, why don't they tell the truth? Have you ever watched them nosing about on Founder's Day? Colonels and doctors and accountants and civil servants, all trying desperately to remember each other's real names because they were called Wally or Cretin or Nickers or something really embarrassing when they were snotty little firsties trying not to blub when they were kissing their mummies goodbye at the beginning of term. Why don't they tell the truth? They's all West Brits of course.
BARRY	West Brits?
CREANEY	You know the sort. Shitting themselves that if the rest of us don't behave the English will get waxy and stop paying their precious salaries. They talk about England as the mainland as if this is some sort of offshore colony.
BARRY	It is.
CREANEY	Listen, Dum Dum, this is where I am and as far as I'm concerned this is the MAIN-LAND! (*Pause. He sings quietly.*) 'And did you see the show, each rose and pink a dilly, O!' To feast your eyes and to view the prize won by the Orange Lily, O!
BARRY	You should have seen the show in the law courts.
CREANEY	(*sings*) The viceroy there, so debonair just like a daffodilly, O!
BARRY	They might as well have been daffodilly O's. Gowns and buckled shoes and wigs. Apparently it all adds to the dignity and solemnity of the judicial process. Right enough it makes them move slowly. They thrust out their chins and frown as if they know they've got to be serious or they'll be ridiculous.

CREANEY   (*posh accent*) Excuse me headmaster, could you
               tell me if there's as much wanking as there was
               in my day? Oh good, good, I'm glad to see the
               traditions of the English public school still
               flourish here in Ulster.

BARRY   Do you know when you become a judge you
               are 'made up'? That's what they say: 'Oh he
               was made up in '74.' They were made up
               alright.

CREANEY   Some day Dum Dum, we'll get out of this hell-
               hole and pick up a couple of big birds and ride
               the arses off them and then we'll swap and do
               it again...some day Dum Dum...some
               day...(*sings*) 'Then come brave boys, and share
               her joys and toast the health of Willy O! Who
               bravely fought on Boyne's red shore the Royal
               Orange Lily, O! Then Heigh heigh ho, the
               Lily O!

               (BARRY *joins in.*)

               The royal loyal Lily O! Beneath the sky

               What flower can vie With Ulster's Orange
               Lily, O!

               (*Black out. Lights come up below on* JAMESON
               dressed as OPHELIA. *He carries a text and is trying to
               learn his lines.*)

JAMESON   'Oh what a noble mind is...is...Oh what a
               noble min...(*He glances at the book and then
               rattles.*) 'Oh what a noble mind is here o'er
               thrown the courtier's soldier's scholar's eye
               tongue sword the expectancy of fashion and
               mould of form the observed of all observers
               quite quite down...'

MRS HOWLETT   (*bustling in with work basket and clothes to add to*
               OPHELIA) I am quite sure the Dean did not tell
               you to say it like that, Jameson.

JAMESON   I'm just learning it, Mrs Howlett.

MRS HOWLETT	Jameson, mein leibling, just slip on this underskirt like a good lad and that will be another beastly little costume out of the way. (*He starts to put it on over his head.*) Jameson not like that...it will end up outside...Oh very well go on now, you dumkof!...My God if there is an awkward way of doing something they will...
	(BARRY *enters and stands watching.*)
	Right down to the ankles, mein schatz, now lift your...(JAMESON *does so, revealing a pair of striped rugby socks.*) STOP!
JAMESON	What, Mrs Howlett?
MRS HOWLETT	What are you wearing on your legs, Jameson?
JAMESON	Rugby socks, Mrs Howlett.
MRS HOWLETT	I can see they are rugby socks, you miscreant. Can you imagine the effect of those gaudy stripes on the audience?
JAMESON	No, Mrs Howlett.
MRS HOWLETT	They will swoon Jameson, they will swoon. We shall have to carry them out in droves, won't we, master Dunham?
BARRY	Yes, Mrs Howlett.
MRS HOWLETT	Well take them off boy, take them off. (*Snatching the book from him.*) Here, Dunham, hear the wretch's lines will you or the Dean will remove his head from his body and I shall have to dress another Ophelia, God forbid!
BARRY	(*as* JAMESON *struggles with his socks*) Where were you?
MRS HOWLETT	'Quite quite down.'
JAMESON	Don't tell me, Dunham, don't tell me...
BARRY	(*prompting*) 'And I.'
JAMESON	'And I of all ladies most deject and wretched.'
MRS HOWLETT	Exactly.

JAMESON	And...and...and...
BARRY	'Sucked.'
MRS HOWLETT	Sucked?
BARRY	Yes.
MRS HOWLETT	Good heavens.
JAMESON	'Sucked the honey of his music vows...'
MRS HOWLETT	Ahhhh.
JAMESON	'Now...now I see the most noble and most...'
MRS HOWLETT	(*swooping with pins, etc.*) Stand still while I deal with this bodice, Jameson.
JAMESON	(*acting with fervour*) 'Most sovereign reason like sweet bells jangled out of time and harsh that unmatched form and feature of blown youth blasted with ecstacy oh woe is me...'
MRS HOWLETT	What have you got in here, Jameson? In your brassière, my child. With what have you stuffed your bra, mein eulenspiegel?
JAMESON	Shuttlecocks, Mrs Howlett.
MRS HOWLETT	*Shuttlecocks?????*
JAMESON	Yes, Mrs Howlett.
MRS HOWLETT	Jameson, you deject and wretched youth, *shuttlecocks?*
JAMESON	I inverted them, Mrs Howlett.
MRS HOWLETT	Jameson you horrible boy, whether you inverted them or not, they will not do!
JAMESON	Sorry, Mrs Howlett.
MRS HOWLETT	I suppose you are to be congratulated on your originality, Jameson.
JAMESON	Thank you, Mrs Howlett.
MRS HOWLETT	Jameson, I was being ironic.
JAMESON	Sorry, Mrs Howlett.

MRS HOWLETT	It's your mother I'm sorry for, Jameson. Well, take them out...you....you...you Hanz Wurtz...Oh look at the creature...here Jameson let me... (*She produces shuttlecocks.*) Just wait till I show these to Howlie.
JAMESON	What will I put in instead Mrs Howlett?
MRS HOWLETT	Rugby socks, much safer, here I'll do it fumbleton, you carry on with your lines.
BARRY	Woe is me.
JAMESON	(*rattling on as* MRS HOWLETT *fills his bra*) 'Woe is me to have seen what I have seen, seen what I see.'
MRS HOWLETT	There, schotzla! Rugby socks plump out quite decently.
	(*The* DEAN *enters.*)
	Ah Dean, you come upon a most intimate scene.
DEAN	Good afternoon, dear lady.
MRS HOWLETT	Come on Jameson, mein liebling, give us a twirl and let the Dean see.
DEAN	Lovely Mrs Howlett. Once again dear lady, you work your magic on the most unprepossessing of objects. Jameson, you're a smasher!
JAMESON	Why can't we have girls for the girl's parts, Mrs Howlett?
MRS HOWLETT	We are very lucky Jameson, mein beister, that Shakespeare wrote his women's parts for young boys, aren't we, Dean?
DEAN	Yes, Mrs Howlett.
MRS HOWLETT	Look. (*She shows him the shuttlecocks.*)
DEAN	Good heavens.
MRS HOWLETT	In his bra, inverted.
DEAN	What we will they be up to next?

Mrs Howlett	Do not ask. The mind boggles. (*Pause.*) Stop looking at me like that, you old roué. You cannot possibly know what I was thinking.
Dean	My dear lady, I protest.
Mrs Howlett	Now, now, now, no more, you must get on with your rehearsal while I watch my handiwork in action.
Dean	Right. Just before the play, isn't it? Ophelia here, I think. (*Placing* Jameson.) That's it.
Mrs Howlett	Jameson, young ladies of Ophelia's class sit with their knees together.
Dean	(*placing* Barry) Hamlet here.
Barry	'Lady shall I lie on your lap?'
Dean	Close close, come on she's your girlfriend, fiancée, and put your head on her knees, that's it, relax!
Jameson	'No my Lord.'
Mrs Howlett	(*inspiration*) Tights, he needs tights!
Barry	'Do you mean country matters?'
Dean	Emphasise Count — ry matters.
Mrs Howlett	It's bawdy, Dunham.
Jameson	What's bawdy, Mrs Howlett?
Mrs Howlett	Bawdy is all right if it is in Shakespeare, Jameson.
Barry	'Do you think I mean count — ry matters?'
Jameson	'I think nothing my Lord.'
Barry	'That's a fine thought to lay between a maiden's legs.'
Mrs Howlett	More bawdy Jameson, here put on these, mein leibling, and we'll see if we can do something about those maiden's legs. (*She advances with tights.*) Carry on, Dean. (*Her efforts are totally disrupting the rehearsal.*)

JAMESON	(*as* MRS HOWLETT *helps him pull on tights*) 'What is my Lord?'
BARRY	'Nothing.'
JAMESON	'You are merry my Lord.'
MRS HOWLETT	Now hold them over your little nicky wickies Jameson, that's it. Dean, I must dash and see what matron is making of Gertrude's night attire, no matter what we do she turns out like Mrs Tiggy Winkle. The mind boggles.
DEAN	Tell her, dear lady, to make it fit for 'The rank sweat of an enseamed bed.'
MRS HOWLETT	I shall do no such thing.
DEAN	I dare you, dear lady.
MRS HOWLETT	Matron is a very strict presbyterian from Ballymena and it is extremely naughty of you to laugh at her, you are a wicked old man.
DEAN	'We are arrant knaves all, believe none of us.'
MRS HOWLETT	(*going*) I won't.
DEAN	'Go thy ways to a nunnery!'
	(MRS HOWLETT *exits trailing a tinkling laugh. The* DEAN, *staring after her, is suddenly immobile.*)
BARRY	'What should a man do but be merry? For look you how cheerfully my mother looks and my father...'
JAMESON	Shhhhhhhh.
BARRY	What?
JAMESON	He's in a stare, the Dean's in a stare. (*Pause. They look at him.*) He fancies the old bat. God she's weird. (*Imitation.*) 'Jameson, my child, this garment may appear embarrassing but I assure you it is highly practical,' and she dangled the bra in front of me.
BARRY	Let's see. (*Pause.* JAMESON *looks at him, and then pulls open his dress pretending to vamp as he does so.*) There. (*Pause.*) Satisfied? (*He does himself up.*) Patterson says I should have insisted on black lace. The shuttlecocks were his idea.

BARRY   Patterson?

JAMESON   Yeah, after games, in the junior changing
             rooms.

BARRY   But Patterson's a senior.

JAMESON   Oh, he's always ragging about in our changing
             room after games. He asked me to show him
             my costume. He made me put it on for him.
             All the others were whistling and leaping about
             like monkeys. Patterson said they were perverts
             and told me to try shuttlecocks in my bra. The
             old bat nearly went spare, didn't she? (*He
             indicates that the* DEAN *is stirring.*)

BARRY   'And my father died within's two hours.'

JAMESON   'Nay, 'tis twice two months, my lord.'

BARRY   'So long? Nay then let the devil...'

             (JAMESON *exits, dragging the props basket with him.
             In the form of a voice over we hear* BARRY *trying out
             the words of his poem. On stage he is trying out the
             words of a Hamlet soliloquy.*)

BARRY   (*in voice over*) Touch...tongue...teeth...touch...
             tongue...touch...touch...*touch*! etc.

             (*synonomously with the voice over*) Melt...melt...
             Melt...melt...melt...melt...melt!

DEAN   (*impatient, shouting*) 'Thaw and resolve itself into
             a dew!'

BARRY   (*dully, sullenly, without effort*) 'Thaw and resolve
             itself into a dew.'

DEAN   What is wrong with you, boy? (*Pause.*)
             Dunham, there is no time for this sulking!
             What is it? Quickly, in a sentence if you
             please!

BARRY   (*belligerently*) I'm withdrawing my poem.

DEAN   *What?*

BARRY   I'm withdrawing my poem from the verse
             competition.

DEAN	Why, in heaven's name?
BARRY	Because it's rubbish!
DEAN	Nonsense, it's a fine poem.
BARRY	It isn't true.
DEAN	I think it is.
BARRY	I can't write about something I don't know!
DEAN	But Dunham, you do know.
BARRY	I don't, I don't.
DEAN	Good God Dunham, you must let me be the judge of that and I am awarding it first prize.
BARRY	Well you can award it to someone else. (*He walks away.*)
DEAN	*Dunham stop!* (BARRY *stops.*) If you move from that spot you will be in serious trouble, Dunham. *I mean it!* (*Pause.*) Now let's stop and think before we do or say something we may regret, let us be rational. This is no way to behave, is it? *Is it?*
BARRY	No, sir.
DEAN	Well, what do you have to say about it?
BARRY	Sorry, sir.
DEAN	Dunham, I don't know what to make of you. You are playing the lead in the end of term play. You are the winner of the verse competition, your father has been made a judge and is to be the guest of honour at Founder's Day, and you behave in this irrational manner.
BARRY	Yes, sir. Sorry, sir.
DEAN	Dunham, I am here to help.
BARRY	I still want to be a day boy, sir.
DEAN	But why? (*Pause.*) You see you are silent. (*Pause.*) Even if I were to back your request out of a simple desire to accede to your wish,

I should have to furnish the headmaster with reasons and the headmaster has set his face against any further drop in boarding numbers. Did you discuss it with your parents?

BARRY	Yes, sir.
DEAN	What did they say?
BARRY	Nothing yet, sir.
DEAN	I shall ask your father to have a word with you on Founder's Day.
BARRY	Yes, sir.

(*Lights come up on* ANGELA. *She is now playing swing ball in a slow motion mime.* BARRY *is composing his poem. He seems to will her to move and she follows the movements of the poem he recites.*)

BARRY   'The twist of her shoulder
The lift of her hair
At the spring of the ball
And the dance of her dress
And the lilt of its hem...
And the lilt of its hem...'

(ANGELA *moves round and round in time to* BARRY'S *poem miming the movements.*)

'And the lilt of its hem
As it sings round her legs
To the tune of her feet
The tap tap tap of her feet
And the swing of her arm,
And the flash of her hair
And the light of her smile
And the spark of her eye
I watch the girl in the garden
In the garden next to mine.'

(*With a great whoop of triumph* CREANEY *dives on* BARRY *from behind and bears him down to the ground. Light on* ANGELA *fades.*)

CREANEY   AHHHHHHHHHHHHHHHHHHHHH!

BARRY	Ah don't.
CREANEY	(*in high good humour*) Caught you at it.
BARRY	What?
CREANEY	Thinking. Thoughts. Intro-bloody-spection!
BARRY	You took me by surprise.
CREANEY	I took myself by surprise this afternoon. Jesus. Oh boy, did I bloody well surprise myself?
BARRY	How?
CREANEY	I got it. The narles. The narly narly narles.
BARRY	You didn't?
CREANEY	I bloody did. In a laurel bush by the side gate. The piece with the fat legs. Laid out on a bed of moss and dead leaves, broken twigs crackling, branches shaking, birds taking flight, the fucking earth moved, Dum Dum!
BARRY	What was it like?
CREANEY	I told you. The earth moved.
BARRY	I mean really like.
CREANEY	Fantastic.
BARRY	Was it really?
CREANEY	Yeah. Oh yeah. I exploded Dum Dum. My senses took over and I experienced refinements of feeling I could not, could not have imagined even in my rarest fantasies. I exploded everywhere.
BARRY	Honestly?
CREANEY	Shooting stars, comets, soaring rockets, we have lift off!
	(*Sings.*)
	'Then come brave boys, and share her joys and toast
	The health of Willy O!

Who bravely won on Boyne's red shore the
    Royal Orange

Lily O!

BARRY	Tell me about if from the beginning.
CREANEY	Well I met her on the road and sort of chatted her up a bit and she said, 'What about it big boy?'
BARRY	Honestly?
CREANEY	Yeah just like that, straight out. Jesus, she doesn't mess about. Well, we ducked through the hedges and into this bush and we sat down and...
BARRY	*And?*
CREANEY	She pulled her knickers off.
BARRY	You didn't?
CREANEY	Didn't what?
BARRY	Pull her knickers off?
CREANEY	No.
BARRY	What happened then?
CREANEY	Well...she...lay...back...and...I...we...frankly I was disappointed, Dum Dum.
BARRY	Disappointed?
CREANEY	I always imagined that I would...it was all over so effing quickly, I hardly noticed.
	(Pause.)
BARRY	At least you got it, got the narles.
CREANEY	There must be ways of...she didn't think much of it either...well she could hardly have noticed except that I had stopped...she kept on moaning and shoving me about...Bloody uncomfortable actually that bit...she kissed me afterwards and called me love and all sorts of shit...she's a cow...a pig...a big fat sow!

(*Pause.*)

BARRY	Did you know that Patterson spends a lot of time ragging in the junior changing room? He went down there to see Jameson's costume.

(CREANEY *puts his arm round* BARRY.)

BARRY	No.
CREANEY	Please, Dum Dum.
BARRY	(*pleading*) No Creaney no.
CREANEY	Ah come on, Dum Dum, come on please.

(*As he pleads, the rest of the* CLASS *begin to chant The Congo as for Founder's Day performance.*)

DEAN	The Congo by Vachel Lindsay.
CLASS	'Fat black bucks in a wine-barrel room,
	Barrel-house kings with feet unstable,
	Sagged and reeled and pounded on the table,
	Pounded on the table.

Then I heard the boom of the blood-lust song
And a thigh-bone beating on a tin-pan gong,
And BLOOD screamed the whistles and the
    fifes of the warriors

Rattle-rattle, rattle-rattle
Bing
Boomlay, boomlay, boomlay BOOM

Boom steal the pygmies,
Boom kill the Arabs,
Boom kill the white men,
Hoo Hoo Hoo.

(*During this* CREANEY *and* DUNHAM *join the* CLASS *and chant the poem.*)

'Mumbo Jumbo will hoo-doo you
Mumbo Jumbo will hoo-doo you
Mumbo Jumbo will hoo-doo you
Mumbo Jumbo will hoo-doo you
Mumbo Jumbo will hoo-doo you

Canes with a brilliant laquer shine
And tall silk hats that were red as wine
And they pranced with their butterfly partners
    there
Coal-black maidens with pearls in the hair
And bells on their ankles and little black-feet

(*Full of brightness, lightness, confidence.*)

CLASS   'Twas a land transfigured, twas a new
             creation
             Oh, a singing wind swept the negro nation
             And through the backwoods clearing flew: –
             Mumbo Jumbo is dead in the jungle
             Never again will he hoo-doo you
             Never again will he hoo-doo you.

DEAN   'Redeemed were the forests, the beasts and the
             men.
             And only the vulture dared again
             By the far, lone mountains of the moon
             To cry, in the silence, the Congo tune

CLASS   Mumbo Jumbo will hoo-doo you
             Mumbo Jumbo will hoo-doo you
             Mumbo Jumbo will hoo-doo you.

             (*Applause. Then* BILL DUNHAM *begins his
             Founder's Day speech standing at a lectern.*)

BILL   …as you all know the motto of this great
             school is *'Haec Memoria Tene'*. If you have
             forgotten? (*Polite laughter from his audience.*) And
             I see you have not, this means, Hold these
             things in your memory. Now as a very junior
             boy I thought this referred to the endings of
             the third declension. (*Polite laughter.*) And I was
             fearful of the terrible retribution that would be
             consequent on my failure to hold these things
             in my memory. (*Polite laughter.*) Of course, as a
             firsty…are they still called firsties, headmaster?
             I see by his nod that some traditions do
             survive. (*Laughter.*) As a firsty I knew
             absolutely nothing and it was when I gained
             the dizzy heights of the second form and
             consequently knew absolutely everything

(*Laughter.*) that I began to realise that the
school motto meant something more profound.
'*Haec Memoria Tene*'. What is it that we should
hold in our memory? Traditions? Certainly the
right traditions should not be forgotten, the
traditions of this school for instance: a regard
for scholarship, good fellowship, fairness,
courage, compassion, manliness, loyalty, all
these things should be remembered and I am
sure they are. But what other traditions? The
traditions of this place, this Ulster. What are
our traditions? Some people might say that
sectarian strife, political obduracy and murder
are our most enduring traditions? I do not
believe that is so. I would list Ulster kindliness,
openness, straightforwardness, the ability to
call a spade a spade and not an agricultural
implement. (*Laughter.*) A sense of humour that
is as in the best of families, uniquely our own.
A certain thrawness, now don't get me wrong,
I do not mean political intransigence, that
failure of imagination and generosity that
obstructs all reasonable compromise; no, I
mean the refusal to throw away our birthright,
our British way of life, everything we hold
dear. On that there can be no compromise; nor
should there be. Of that way we can properly
use the old war cry, 'No surrender'. (*Polite
clapping and discreet cries of hear hear.*) *Tenete!* I use
the plural imperative because I refer to all of
you. *Tenete!* Hold these thing in your memory!
Remember your duty all of you, for you are
privileged. You are privileged in your homes,
your backgrounds, your friends, your teachers
and above all in your school. You owe all of
these a debt of gratitude. I can quote you
another motto, the motto of this great City:
'*Pro Tanto Quid Retibuamus*'. For so much what
will we give back. You are the leaders of the
next generation. Your province languishes; it
cries out for leadership as never before:
leadership in industry, in medicine, in the law,
in the Church and above all in politics.

We, the older generation, need YOU! *Haec Memoria Tenete!*

(*Black out. The boys cross the stage and remove the lectern.*)

BUTLER	How long was it?
LOWRY	19 minutes and 40 seconds.
ROBINSON	Is that all?
DUNBAR	Seemed a lot longer.
BUTLER	Longest speech I ever heard.
BOBBY	Anybody guess it?
RICHARDS	I did.

(PATTERSON *enters.*)

BOBBY	Hey Patterson, Wombat's won.
RICHARDS	19 minutes and 40 seconds.
PATTERSON	That is within the stipulated limit.
RICHARDS	Well, pay up.
PATTERSON	Where's your ticket?
RICHARDS	What ticket?
PATTERSON	I gave everyone a ticket.
RICHARDS	But you wrote it down.
PATTERSON	(*exiting*) No ticket, no pay out!
DUNBAR	Wombat, Wombat your prize wally...
BOYS	(*exiting*) Wally, idiot etc., etc...
RICHARDS	(*following and shouting*) I didn't know you had to keep the ticket. You wrote it down.

(BILL *and* BARRY *enter.*)

BILL	...'just a feeling' does not satisfy the rules of evidence you know.
BARRY	I know that I...

BILL   The Dean informs me that the headmaster has
            set his face against any further drop in the
            boarding numbers.

BARRY   I know but...

BILL   So even if he and I were persuaded that you
            had good reason for becoming a day boy there
            is little we could do about it. You do see that?

BARRY   Yes.

BILL   You would have to change schools and I would
            look pretty silly advocating that course of
            action after the speech I have just made.
            Wouldn't I?

BARRY   Yes.

BILL   Besides it is much safer than you going in and
            out of the house everyday.

BARRY   Yes.

            (*The* DEAN *enters.*)

DEAN   Ah Bill...marvellous speech.

BILL   Thank you, Dean.

DEAN   The traditions of this place, this Ulster?

BILL   The best traditions.

DEAN   It had a sort of...a sort of...tough
            reasonableness.

BILL   Calling a spade a spade perhaps?

DEAN   And not a...(*Laughs.*) That's the Ulsterman I
            know, the Ulsterman I can and do respect.

BILL   Well, he does exist you know.

DEAN   Oh God, Bill, I do wish they'd see sense.

BILL   Yes.

DEAN   They can be so expasperating.

BILL   Some of the wilder ones end up before me in
            court.

DEAN	Of course. (*Pause.* DEAN *smiles at him. A favourite old boy.*) I'm so glad the boys heard you. Do them good. *Haec memoria tene.*
BILL	*Pro tanto quid retribuamus.*
DEAN	Yes. Yes indeed. Well, how's this young man?
BILL	Well...we've been discussing things...haven't we, Barry?
BARRY	Yes.
DEAN	Any conclusions?
BILL	Weighing up the evidence, I think. Eh, Barry?
BARRY	Yes.
BILL	Logically and calmly making up our mind.
DEAN	Feel like a leader of tomorrow, Barry!
BARRY	(*horrified*) No!
DEAN	Your province cries out for leadership...it languishes.
BILL	Don't tease him.
DEAN	Well, how if we try out his potential on the house first?
BILL	An apprenticeship?
DEAN	I always make at least one new prefect this term; when the A levels start and the present leadership is *hors de combat.* as it were...well, Barry?
BILL	What do you say to that, Barry?
	(MRS HOWLETT *sweeps in with* MARION *in tow.*)
MRS HOWLETT	Lovely speech Bill, lovely, just right for these difficult times. Howlie will be along in a minute; dealing with an awkward parent. Ballymena man. (*She makes a truly awful attempt at a Ballymena accent.*) 'I dunna thunk are wee Wullie's being praperly straitched Mr Howlett Surrr.' (*They laugh.*) Our 'Wullie', God bless

him, is as thick as two short planks. Can't tell
that to Ballymena man. Ballymena màn as
thick as three short planks. (*They laugh.*)
Ballymena woman is non est. How do you talk
to a family that consists entirely of five short
planks? You have to converse with them in
code. Howlie's good at code; that's why they
made him headmaster! (*Laughter.*) Drinks
through this way. (*The men follow her off.*
MARION *lingers to talk to* BARRY.)

MARION   Well?

BARRY   Well what?

MARION   Did you and Daddy...did you...

BARRY   Yes!

             (*Pause.*)

MARION   (*put off by his vehemence she tries a different tack*)
             Did you enjoy Daddy's speech?

BARRY   NO!

             (*She is alarmed.*)

             It was rubbish!

MARION   I hope you didn't tell him.

BARRY   Of course not. Do you think I'm mad?

MARION   Well, ever since that outburst in the law courts
             Barry, I...

BARRY   *I apologised for that!*

MARION   I know Barry, I...

BARRY   Anyway it wasn't an outburst, I just asked if I
             could become a day boy; that's not an
             outburst, is it?

MARION   The timing Barry?

BARRY   *I apologised didn't I?*

MARION   I know you apologised.

BARRY   *Well don't go on about it then!*

MARION   Barry love, don't be so rude!

BARRY	SORRY! (*Pause.*) Sorry sorry sorry, it's all I ever bloody say these days.
MARION	Barry, love.
BARRY	Creaney's right.
MARION	Who's Creaney?
BARRY	A friend of mine.
MARION	Why is he right?
BARRY	No one tells the truth. Why don't they tell the truth?
MARION	The truth about what, Barry love?
BARRY	This place. Here. Us. Themselves.
MARION	Barry?
BARRY	I have to go!
MARION	Barry love?
BARRY	Goodbye. (*He exits.*)
MARION	You will see us before...
	(*But he is gone. The* DEAN, BILL *and* MRS HOWLETT *enter with drinks.* MRS HOWLETT *has a sherry for* MARION)
MRS HOWLETT	Bill said a medium dry sherry was your tipple, Marion dear.
MARION	Oh, thanks...
BILL	Where's Barry?
MARION	Oh...he said he had to go somewhere...he went...
DEAN	You can have a word later, Bill.
MRS HOWLETT	After dinner.
DEAN	Before you go.
MARION	I think perhaps he was a bit...
BILL	The Dean is going to make him a prefect.
MARION	Oh...wonderful.

MRS HOWLETT   He's one of the nicest boys in the school,
               Marion.

MARION   Oh thank...

BILL   I'm surprised he didn't mention it.

MARION   What?

BILL   The prefectship?

MARION   Oh...

BILL   What did he say?

MARION   Oh...he ah...he talked about a friend of
               his...called Creaney.

MRS HOWLETT   Oh my God the gorilla from Armagh!

DEAN   Now dear lady, you speak of one of our
               brightest boys.

MRS HOWLETT   Bright he may be Dean, but politically and
               socially he's a gorilla. (*Leading them off.*) Do you
               know he told me that he was one of the ancient
               people of Ulster? I said, 'Creaney, with
               opinions like yours you probably are, you
               probably are! (*They leave, laughing.*)

BARRY   (*enters and tries to make his poem*) Touch...
               tongue...lips...teeth...teeth...pearl...p...p...
               p...pearl...

               (ANGELA *enters and circles him. She goes very close.
               He is transfixed, mesmerised, her face is close to his as
               if she is about to kiss him.*)

               Pearl...lipssss...kisssss...kisss...

               (*But she goes and his final words cannot bring her
               back.* JAMESON, *in his Ophelia costume, drags on the
               props basket, sits on it and reads a book.* BARRY
               joins him.)

JAMESON   (*sniggering*) There's lots more of it. Stacks and
               stacks of it. Shakespeare must have been a
               dirty old bugger. I have to say cock.

BARRY   Well?

JAMESON   Listen, listen. (*He turns the pages of his book.*)

BARRY   What's that?

JAMESON   A book on bawdy. 'It's all right if it's in
             Shakespeare, mein leibling', here it is: COCK.
             Male domestic fowl hence applied to objects
             resembling same, such as cock short for water
             cock or tap thus meaning penis not only from
             the shape but from the fact a penis emits water
             and sperm. (*He giggles.*) Tumble — I have to
             say tumble...R — S — T...(BARRY *moves
             closer.*) Tail...Jesus you want to read tail
             and...THING...God 'thing'...I mean who
             would have thought of 'thing'...and 'take' and
             'taste' and 'tickle'!...You know everything is
             sex, everything...It's dreadful...God, it's
             awful...Here. 'Tumble.' To cause to fall
             backwards, to copulate...that's the narles isn't
             it?

BARRY   Yes.

JAMESON   (*trying out the word*) Cop-U-late. 'Quoth she,
             before you tumbled me, you promised me to
             wed.' I have to say that...

             (BARRY *lifts a fold of his dress and runs it through
             his hand.*)

BARRY   It's not satin only poly-what's-it. 'Jameson,
             you dumkopf, when I watch you running down
             stairs in your dress I thank God for synthetic
             fibres.'

             (*Pause.*)

JAMESON   Why are you staring at me, Dunham?

BARRY   (*looking away, guiltily*) I'm not.

JAMESON   I don't mind. Stare away. Patterson says I
             have a glad eye. He stares at me all the time.

             (*sings*) 'By Gis and by St Charity,
             Alack and fie for shame!'

             Did you ever hear such rot? Of course I'm
             mad by this stage.

(*sings*) 'Young men will do it if they come to it.
By cock they are to blame.
Quoth she, before you tumbled me,
You promised me to wed.'

(*Pause.* BARRY *has put his arm round his shoulder.*)

Hey?

BARRY What?

JAMESON Let go. (BARRY *takes his arm away.*) I have to
see the old Bat. 'Shoes Jameson, where am I
expected to get shoes for such feet!' (*Drags off
the props basket leaving the book behind.*)

BARRY (*reading book*) 'Incline'...disposed to love
making...'Itch'...fugitive amorous
desire...'Ireland'...the urinary and defecatory
organs of women.

(BILL *appears beside him, wearing a coat.*)

BILL   Well Barry?

BARRY Yes?

BILL   Thought it over?

BARRY Yes.

(*Pause.*)

BILL   Would you like me to...sum up. (*He smiles
hopefully.*) The plaintiff...alleges that sometimes
school is, quote 'too much for him.' He
summarises his objections as 'just a feeling'.
The defendant...to extend the judicial
metaphor...the defendant argues that if the
plaintiff plays his cards right and ceases
withdrawing his poems from the competition
he has already won on the grounds that they
are, quote 'rubbish', the plaintiff will be head
of house and in a mere eighteen months off to
univ...

BARRY (*shouting*) ALRIGHT!

BILL   Barry?

BARRY   *I agree. I agree. I bloody well agree. Stop bloody
                 going on and on about it!*

                 (*Long pause.*)

BILL   Barry, you cannot take a decision in this frame
                 of mind.

BARRY   (*sullenly*) What frame of mind?

BILL   You know.

BARRY   No I don't!

BILL   You have lost your temper.

BARRY   *No I haven't!*

BILL   But this display of childish and emotional fury
                 demonstrates clearly that you have.

BARRY   You all treat me as a child.

BILL   But as soon as you react like a reasonable and
                 rational adult you will be treated as one.

BARRY   Why must everything be reasonable and
                 rational? WHY? Maybe things aren't! Maybe
                 they're confused and dark and sudden and
                 bloody and fierce and terrible...

BILL   (*reaching out a hand to touch him*) Barry? Barry?

BARRY   *Leave me alone! Leave me alone!*

                 (*He runs off.*)

BILL   (*shouting*) *Barry!*

                 (BILL *exits.* JAMESON *runs across the stage and*
                 CREANEY *enters.*)

CREANEY   Hey Jameson, have you see Dunham?

JAMESON   Yes.

CREANEY   Where?

JAMESON	None of your business.
CREANEY	(*grabbing his arm and twisting it behind his back*)
	Where is he, you cheeky wee shit? Tell me. Tell me.
JAMESON	Achhhhhhhhh. Creaney, let me go! I have a rehearsal! (*The pain is too great.*) He was in the changing room!
CREANEY	The junior changing room?
JAMESON	Yes.
CREANEY	(*twisting*) You're a liar.
JAMESON	I'm not, I'm not, I'm not, I swear I'm not! (CREANEY *lets him go.*) Creaney, that hurt. You nearly broke my arm.
CREANEY	Stop moaning.
JAMESON	It's alright for you to say stop moaning, it's not your arm.
CREANEY	Dunham went to the junior changing room to fetch you for rehearsals, didn't he?
JAMESON	No he bloody didn't.
CREANEY	Well what did..?(*He tails off.*)
JAMESON	If you really want to know, he tried to kiss me.
CREANEY	(*grabbing his arm and twisting again*) What did you say?
JAMESON	(*crying out in pain*) He tried to kiss me!
CREANEY	(*twisting viciously*) You're a liar!
JAMESON	I'm not, I'm not, I'm not, I ammmmmmmmm (CREANEY *releases him.*) I'm not though. He tried to kiss me and then ran off. He's gay and I'm going to tell!
CREANEY	You open your mouth you filthy little flirt...
	(*But* JAMESON *flees as* PATTERSON *enters.*)
PATTERSON	Strong words, Creaney.

CREANEY	What's it to you, Patterson?
PATTERSON	Intriguing though. 'Filthy little flirt?'. Now who was he flirting with? Your sister? Hardly likely since your sister, if you have one, is some culchie wench from darkest Armagh...
CREANEY	Shut your face, Patterson!
PATTERSON	Oh dear, oh dear we are in a passion, all in a muck sweat, and Jameson running off, his skirts flying about his ankles...
	(*Creaney hits him in the stomach and he doubles up with a groan. He hits him again and he goes down. The* DEAN *enters from the direction in which* JAMESON *fled.*)
DEAN	Creaney?
CREANEY	(*swinging round*) Yes, sir?
DEAN	Do you know where Dunham is?
CREANEY	No, sir. (*Pause.*) Is anything wrong, sir?
DEAN	(*calmly*) I am afraid it is Creaney, I am afraid something is very wrong. (*Considering.*) Look Creaney this is a...delicate matter...I would, however, value your co-operation.
CREANEY	Yes, sir.
DEAN	I need to find Dunham quickly...and if possible discreetly. I don't want any fuss, no hue and cry, do you understand, boy?
CREANEY	Jameson's an awful little liar, sir.
DEAN	What?
CREANEY	He exaggerates, sir.
DEAN	Creaney, what are you talking about?
CREANEY	Explaining why Dunham ran off, sir.
DEAN	(*alarmed*) Why did he run off?
CREANEY	Because...
DEAN	Why, Creaney?

CREANEY	Because he...he was upset, sir.
DEAN	Upset? Does he know?
CREANEY	Know what, sir?
DEAN	His father is dead, Creaney. Shot dead. Assassinated. Terrorists. I am relying on your discretion, Creaney. You're a friend of his. We've got to find him.
CREANEY	I think I know where he might be, sir.
DEAN	Where?
CREANEY	(*pointing*) Up there, sir.
DEAN	In the roof space?
CREANEY	Yes.

(BARRY *is in fact moving onto his crossbeam*)

DEAN	Why up there?
CREANEY	He goes there...when something has upset him, sir.

(*Pause. They both look up.*)

DEAN	Dunham! Dunham! Dunham, are you up there?

(BARRY *cringes back.*)

I think something moved. Dunham is that you? (*Quietly.*) Can you get him down?

CREANEY	I'll try. (*He runs off.*)

(PATTERSON *has for some time been trying to attract attention to himself by groaning where he lies.*)

DEAN	(*furiously*) What are you doing down there?
PATTERSON	Sir, Creaney, sir...
DEAN	Oh, for heavens sake get up boy and stand on your feet! Dunham? Dunham? Dunham old chap, do be sensible and come down.

(PATTERSON *gets painfully to his feet.*)

MRS HOWLETT	(*entering*) Dean? Ah Dean, there you are?

DEAN	Shhhhhhhh.
MRS HOWLETT	What?
DEAN	Shhhh. (*Pause.*) Dunham?
MRS HOWLETT	(*whisper*) How did he know?
DEAN	I don't know.
MRS HOWLETT	Dunham! Dunham, it's Mrs Howlett.

(*Pause.* CREANEY *is on the beam a bit away from* BARRY.)

CREANEY	Dum Dum? (*Pause.*) Dum Dum?
BARRY	Go away!
CREANEY	No look…
BARRY	(*at extreme and dangerous edge*) Don't come any closer!
CREANEY	(*alarmed*) I won't, I won't!
DEAN	Dunham!
MRS HOWLETT	Barry? Barry?

(*In ones and twos the rest of the* CLASS *begin to collect below, whisper together and watch.*)

DEAN	Is he there, Creaney? Creaney?
MRS HOWLETT	Creaney, is Barry there?
DEAN	Have you found him, Creaney?
CREANEY	YES!
BARRY	(*hissed*) Lundy!
CREANEY	No, Dum Dum, look…
BARRY	Lundy! Judas!
CREANEY	It's not what you think.
MRS HOWLETT	Barry?
DEAN	Is he all right, Creaney?
CREANEY	It's not about Jameson.
BARRY	What do you know about Jameson? What did he tell you?

CREANEY	Nothing, nothing!
BARRY	How do you know then? How? You do know, don't you?
CREANEY	Yes but look...
BARRY	And they sent you. Didn't they? Didn't they? DIDN'T THEY?
CREANEY	YES!
BARRY	Judas. Lundy.
DEAN	Dunham your father wouldn't want this, you know?

(*Barry groans, topples.*)

MRS HOWLETT	Barry dear, think of your mother. Think of what she...
CREANEY	SHUT UP!
MRS HOWLETT	What?
CREANEY	FOR JESUS CHRIST'S SAKE SHUT YOUR MOUTH YOU STUPID OLD BAT!
DEAN	(*horrified*) CREANEY!
CREANEY	YOU SHUT UP TOO YOU OUL SHITE!

(*Pause. The* DEAN *and* MRS HOWLETT *look at each other in silence.*)

They don't know anything. I swear.

BARRY	Why are they looking for me then?
CREANEY	Your father...(*Pauses.*)
BARRY	He's not here, is he? IS HE?
CREANEY	NO! (*Pause.*) No, Dum Dum, he's not here.
BARRY	I can't face him.
CREANEY	He'll never know.
BARRY	Why not?
CREANEY	Come away from the edge and I'll tell you.

	(CREANEY *is creeping closer: pieces of ceiling begin to fall.*)
DEAN	Creaney, what is going on up there?
BARRY	Why will my father never know?
CREANEY	Come away from the edge.
BARRY	Why?
DEAN	CREANEY!
CREANEY	Because...because...
BARRY	WHY?
MRS HOWLETT	Barry!
CREANEY	Come off that beam and I'll tell you!
	(*More ceiling falls.*)
DEAN	CREANEY!
BARRY	TELL ME!
MRS HOWLETT	Barry!
CREANEY	Because...because...
BARRY	TELL ME DAMN YOU!
CREANEY	Because he's dead. (*He grabs* BARRY *and together they rock on the beam.* CREANEY'S *arms round him. Bits of the ceiling cascade down. Beam blacked out.* MRS HOWLETT *screams. The* CLASS *have collected round* PATTERSON.)
DUNBAR	Murdering bastards!
BUTLER	IRA scum!
DEAN	(DEAN *turns towards them*) I think you should all go back. The bell for tea you should all...
DUNBAR	FILTH!
	(*Led by* DUNBAR *the class goes beserk, chanting and shouting 'IRA bastards' etc.*)
DEAN	The bell has gone!
	(*But the riot continues and the* DEAN *shouts and waves his stick.*)
	STOP!
	(*The boys back down, sullenly.* DUNBAR *last.*)

DEAN   Now boys, the way to deal with this is to go about our everyday affairs as if nothing has happened. It is the object of terror to disrupt life. Now we best serve gallant man like Bill Dunham, and his son your classmate, by carrying on as normal.

            (*Quietly the boys file off in ordered rows. The* DEAN'*s desk is brought on. The* DEAN *turns and is speaking to* BARRY *at his desk.* BARRY *has a small suitcase.*)

DEAN   ...and of course there is your mother, you have got to think of her, for your own sake as well as her's. You must be the man in the house. Comfort her Barry, and allow her to comfort you. She may want to overcomfort you, so be tolerant.

BARRY   Yes, sir.

DEAN   I shall be sorry to lose you from the house but there...there...there...

            (*The* DEAN *goes into a stare.* BARRY *passes his hand in front of his face then picks up his case and leaves.* DEAN *comes out of his stare and exits. Boys remove desk.* MARION *enters, wearing an apron.*)

MARION   (*calling to* BARRY *off stage*) Steak and kidney pie dear! Your favourite. There was sole in the fishmongers but the man of the house must have what he likes. (*Pause.*) leave the unpacking Barry, I'll do it after dinner. (*Pause.*) I thought we might go for a drive tomorrow, if you like. You can do the driving. There was that funny place you wanted to see. The Black Crow...no the Black Pig, was that it, dear?

BARRY   (*entering*) The Black Pig's dyke.

MARION   (*busy, not looking at him yet*) That was it. Why do you want to go there?

BARRY   I want to see it for myself.

MARION   Oh I thought we could go together.

BARRY	I didn't mean that. I just meant seeing it. For myself. There are other places I want to see too.
MARION	(*looking at him now*) Well of course, dear.
BARRY	I need to make up my own mind about them.
MARION	(*puzzled*) Yes dear.
BARRY	And other things. I need to make up my own mind about everything.
MARION	You've changed.
BARRY	Have I?
MARION	Jeans.
BARRY	Oh.
MARION	The pie won't be long, I put an egg in it, just for you. Would you like to eat in here or in the dining room?
BARRY	I don't mind.
MARION	Well you say dear, I always asked...
BARRY	You always asked Daddy?
MARION	Yes.
BARRY	I don't mind.
MARION	Well alright, we'll have it in here it's not so formal, more cosy, but then I thought maybe on your first night perhaps...(*She suddenly grabs him and sobs.*) Oh Barry, Barry...(*Pulling herself together.*) sorry...sorry...I promised myself I wouldn't...
BARRY	(*gently*) It's alright. I don't mind.
MARION	Thank you. Thank you. Dinner won't be long. Would you like to join me in a sherry?
BARRY	No thanks.
MARION	It's a very good sherry your father...it's very good.
BARRY	No thanks.

MARION	I shall feel odd drinking on my own. Bad sign. Sure you won't?
BARRY	No thanks, Mum.
MARION	Well I won't either then.
BARRY	No, you go ahead.
MARION	Where are you going?
BARRY	(*leaving*) Into the garden.
MARION	Well don't be too long, dear.

(BARRY *turns away. The fence comes on.* ANGELA *plays swing ball on the other side.*)

BARRY	Hey!
ANGELA	Hello. One hundred and twenty-one, one hundred and twenty-two, etc.
BARRY	Can I have a go?
ANGELA	Yes alright.
BARRY	Look out I'm coming over.

(*He takes a run at the fence fails to cross it and ends up stuck half way.* ANGELA *laughs. He falls back.*) I thought I could...

ANGELA	Have you hurt yourself?
BARRY	(*ruefully examining an elbow*) No.
ANGELA	(*pointing to the bottom of the fence*) There's a gap here. Of course you go out of your garden and into the road and come in by the gate like ordinary people.
BARRY	No, I'll try here.

(*He squirms and grunts his way through a hole in the bottom of the fence but comes to an undignified halt half way through.*)

ANGELA	(*reaching out her hands*) Here.
BARRY	Thanks.
ANGELA	Wait! Your jumper's caught.

BARRY	It's all right.
ANGELA	Keep still you eejit, you'll ruin it. No, push yourself back with your hands. That's it. You're free. (*He slithers through the gap on his stomach.*)
BARRY	Wheeeeeeee.
ANGELA	Like a snake. A very clumsy snake. You're all clay. Let me brush it off. There.
BARRY	Thanks. Lend me the racquet.
ANGELA	Here.
	(BARRY *has a go and manages a few feeble thwacks. She laughs. He laughs too, jumping around in idiot fashion.*) You're hopeless.
BARRY	You've had practice.
ANGELA	Here let me show you. Give me the racquet. Come on.
	(*He stands holding the racquet.*) Come on. The racquet.
BARRY	Give me a kiss first.
	(*Pause. Then quickly she kisses him on the cheek and tries to grab the racquet but instead he grips her shoulders and kisses her on the lips. Again. They part.*)
ANGELA	It's time for my tea.
BARRY	Oh.
ANGELA	Give me the racquet please.
BARRY	Oh. (*He hands it to her.*)
ANGELA	You can go out of the gate, if you like.
BARRY	Right.
ANGELA	I must go in.
BARRY	Right.
ANGELA	Goodbye.

BARRY   Good...WAIT!

ANGELA   (*turning*) What?

BARRY   What's your name?

ANGELA   Angela.

BARRY   Mine's Barry.

ANGELA   I know.

             (*Pause.*)

ANGELA   Bye.

BARRY   WAIT!

ANGELA   What?

BARRY   Can I see you tomorrow?

ANGELA   Yes. (*Pause.*) Bye. (*He exits.*)

BARRY   (*Long pause. Quietly*) Boomlay, boomlay,
             boomlay, boom. (*He laughs and he chuckles
             exhultantly.*) Boom, boom, boom. (*He laughs
             again.*) Kissing is nothing...kissing's...
             everything. Boomlay, boomlay, boomlay,
             boom. (*Louder.*) Mumbo Jumbo is dead in the
             jungle. Never again will he hoodoo you!
             (*Exhultant now, a great chant of joy and freedom, and
             a wild dance to go with it.*) Mumbo Jumbo is
             dead in the jungle, never again will he hoo-doo
             you, hoo-doo you, never again will he hoo-doo
             you. (*Laughter slowly dying away. Quietly now, very
             still.*)

Mumbo jumbo is dead in the jungle, dead in the jungle I'm glad... you're dead in the jungle, glad you're dead in the jungle, dead in the jungle, dead in the jungle (*Bursting into uncontrollable sobbing.*) dead in the jungle, dead in the jungle, I'm glad you're dead in the jungle. (*Through gritted teeth and with clenched fist*) Then I saw the congo, creeping through the black, cutting through the forest with a golden track. Boomlay Boomlay Boomlay Boom! Boomlay Boomlay Boomlay — (*He vaults the fence, landing on the far side with the final*) Boom!

END.

THE CONGO
A Study of the Negro Race
Being a memorial to Ray Eldred, a Disciple missionary of the Congo River

I. Their Basic Savagery

Fat black bucks in a wine-barrel room,
Barrel-house kings, with feet unstable,
Sagged and reeled and pounded on the table,
Pounded on the table,
Beat an empty barrel with the handle of a broom,
Hard as they were able,
Boom, boom, BOOM,
With a silk umbrella and the handle of a broom,
Boomlay, boomlay, boomlay, BOOM
THEN I had religion, THEN I had a vision.
I could not turn from their revel in derision.
THEN I SAW THE CONGO, CREEPING THROUGH THE BLACK.
CUTTING THROUGH THE FOREST WITH A GOLDEN TRACK.
Then along that riverbank
A thousand miles
Tattooed cannibals danced in files;
Then I heard the boom of the blood-lust song
And a thigh-bone beating on a tin-pan gong.
And "BLOOD" screamed the whistles and the fifes of the
    warriors,
"BLOOD" screamed the skull-faced, lean witch-doctors,
"Whirl ye the deadly voo-doo rattle,
Harry the uplands,
Steal all the cattle,
Rattle-rattle, rattle-rattle,
Bing.
Boomlay, boomlay, boomlay, BOOM,"
A roaring, epic, rag-time tune
From the mouth of the Congo
To the Mountains of the Moon.
Death is an Elephant,
Torch-eyed and horrible,
Foam-flanked and terrible.
BOOM, steal the pygmies,
BOOM, kill the Arabs,

BOOM, kill the white men,
Hoo, Hoo, Hoo.

Listen to the yell of Leopold's ghost
Burning in Hell for his hand-maimed host.
Hear how the demons chuckle and yell
Cutting his hands off, down in Hell.
Listen to the creepy proclamation.
Blown through the lairs of the forest-nation,
Blown past the white-ants' hill of clay,
Blown past the marsh where the butterflies play:—
"Be careful what you do,
Or Mumbo-Jumbo, God of the Congo,
And all of the other
Gods of the Congo,
Mumbo-Jumbo will hoo-doo you,
Mumbo-Jumbo will hoo-doo you,
Mumbo-Jumbo will hoo-doo you."

II. Their Irrepressible High Spirits
Wild crap-shooters with a whoop and a call
Danced the juba in their gambling hall
And laughed fit to kill, and shook the town,
And guyed the policemen and laughed them down
With a boomlay, boomlay, boomlay, BOOM.
THEN I SAW THE CONGO, CREEPING THROUGH THE BLACK.
CUTTING THROUGH THE FOREST WITH A GOLDEN TRACK.
A Negro fairyland swung into view,
A minstrel river
Where dreams come true.
The ebony palace soared on high
Through the blossoming trees to the evening sky.
The inlaid porches and casements shone
With gold and ivory and elephant-bone.
And the black crowd laughed till their sides were sore
At the baboon butler in the agate door,
And the well-known tunes of the parrot band
That trilled on the bushes of that magic land.

A troupe of skull-faced witch-men came
Through the agate doorway in suits of flame,
Yea, long-tailed coats with a gold-leaf crust
And hats that were covered with diamond-dust.

And the crowd in the court gave a whoop and a call
And danced the juba from wall to wall.
But the witch-men suddenly stilled the throng
With a stern cold glare, and a stern old song:—
"Mumbo-Jumbo will hoo-doo you."...
Just then from the doorway, as fat as shotes,
Came the cake-walk princes in their long red coats,
Canes with a brilliant lacquer shine,
And tall silk hats that were red as wine,
And they pranced with their butterfly partners there,
Coal-black maidens with pearls in their hair,
Knee-skirts trimmed with the jassamine sweet,
And bells on their ankles and little black-feet.
And the couples railed at the chant and frown
Of the witch-men lean, and laughed them down.
(Oh, rare was the revel, and well worth while
That made those glowering witch-men smile.)

The cake-walk royalty then began
To walk for a cake that was tall as a man
To the tune of "Boomlay, boomlay, BOOM,"
While the witch-men laughed, with a sinister air,
And sang with the scalawags prancing there:—
"Walk with care, walk with care,
Or Mumbo-Jumbo, God of the Congo,
And all of the other Gods of the Congo,
Mumbo-Jumbo will hoo-doo you.
Beware, beware, walk with care,
Boomlay, boomlay, boomlay, boom.
Boomlay, boomlay, boomlay, boom.
Boomlay, boomlay, boomlay, boom.
Boomlay, boomlay, boomlay,
BOOM
(Oh, rare was the revel, and well worth while
That made those glowering witch-men smile.)

III. The Hope of Their Religion
A good old Negro in the slums of the town
Preached at a sister for her velvet gown.
Howled at a brother for his low-down ways,
His prowling, guzzling, sneak-thief days.
Beat on the Bible till he wore it out

Starting the jubilee revival shout.
And some had visions, as they stood on chairs,
And sang of Jacob, and the golden stairs,
And they all repented, a thousand strong
From their stupor and savagery and sin and wrong
And slammed with their hymm books till they shook the room
With "glory, glory, glory,"
And "Boom, boom, Boom."
THEN I SAW THE CONGO, CREEPING THROUGH THE BLACK,
CUTTING THROUGH THE JUNGLE WITH A GOLDEN TRACK.
And the gray sky opened like a new-rent veil
And showed the Apostles with their coats of mail.
In bright white steel they were seated round
And their fire-eyes watched where the Congo wound.
And the twelve Apostles, from their thrones on high
Thrilled all the forest with their heavenly cry:—
"Mumbo-Jumbo will die in the jungle;
Never again will he hoo-doo you.
Never again will be hoo-doo you."

Then along that river, a thousand miles
The vine-snared trees fell down in files.
Pioneer angels cleared the way
For a Congo paradise, for babes at play,
For sacred capitals, for temples clean.
Gone were the skull-faced witch-men lean.
There, where the wild ghost-gods had wailed
A million boats of the angels sailed
With oars of silver, and prows of blue
And silken pennants that the sun shone through.
'Twas a land transfigured, 'twas a new creation.
Oh, a singing wind swept the negro nation
And on through the backwoods clearing flew:—
"Mumbo-Jumbo is dead in the jungle.
Never again will he hoo-doo you.
Never again will he hoo-doo you.

Redeemed were the forests, the beasts and the men,
And only the vulture dared again
By the far, lone mountains of the moon
To cry, in silence, the Congo tune:—
Mumbo-Jumbo will hoo-doo you,

"Mumbo-Jumbo will hoo-doo you.
Mumbo ... Jumbo ... will ... hoo-doo ... you."

This poem, particularly the third section, was suggested by an allusion in a sermon by my pastor, F.W. Burnham, to the heroic life and death of Ray Eldred. Eldred was a missionary of the Disciples of Christ who perished while swimming a treacherous branch of the Congo.

PLAN OF ROBING ROOM TABLE LAYOUT

a. Green writing pad

b. Silver tray with mirror & brush

c. Ink well

d. Wig tin with lid open and FULL-BOTTOMED wig facing onstage

e. Black belt

f. Black stoll

g. Red gun case

h. Red cape with lining face up, back scrunched up & tail on top (Cape lying on front) Ties undone.

i. Fur trimmed cloak lying on top of cape

j. White handkerchief

k. Black handkerchief (Death)

l. White gloves

m. Top hat (To come)

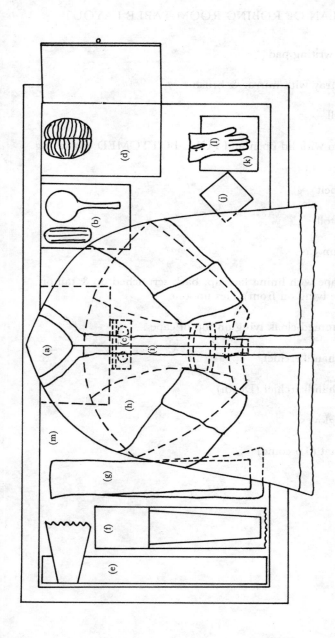

PROPERTY LIST

FURNITURE

10 school chairs
Teacher's desk and chair
3 canvas chairs; one with 'director' on back
2 wicker hampers
Study chair
Study armchair
Study bookcase
Swing ball and garden fence
Double bed, made
Ottoman
Cheval mirror
3 robing room chairs
Robing room table
Lectern
2 chairs (court scene)

Act One

2 walking sticks (The Dean)
Waste paper basket
On teacher's desk: blackboard rubber
                  chalk box with chalks
                  6 essays
                  3 English text books
On each school desk: photocopies of sections of 'The Congo',
                  pages 1 – 3 in script
Rugby ball (Creany)
2 maracas (Richards)
Hand written copy of short poem with one verse by Barry
   (Dean)
Dunham's Hamlet costume (Mrs Howlett)
Jewelled cricket box (Mrs Howlett)
Swingball racquet (Angela)
Five pound note (Dunbar)
Hand written copy of long poem with two verses by Barry
   (Dean)
Exeat (Dean)

Act Two

On double bed: Dress (Marion Dunham)
                  3 assorted hats (Marion)
                  2 clutch bags (Marion)
                  1 pair of gloves (Marion)
                  Woman's magazine
                  Pair ladies tights
                  Packet of tights, unopened
                  Ladies comb

On robing room table: *see plan of robing room table*
                  Writing blotter
                  Silver tray with clothes brush and hand
                     mirror
                  Ink well
                  Wig tin, open, and full-bottomed wig
                  Black belt
                  Black stoll
                  Red gun case
                  Red cape with lining face up, back
                     scrunched up and tail on top, ties
                     undone
                  Fur trimmed cloak, lying on top of cape
                  White handkerchief
                  Black handkerchief—death
                  Pair of white gloves
                  Top hat (Clerk)

Cricket bat (Lowry)
2 cricket caps (Lowry)
Cricket jumper (Lowry)
2 cricket pads (Lowry)
Cricket bag with glove hanging out of pocket (Lowry)
2 cricket balls (McKenna and Richards)
3 Hamlet text paperbacks (Jameson, Barry, Dean)
3 plastic carrier bags containing assorted tights and Jameson's
   Ophelia tights; assorted underslips; assorted material
   oddments
Costume rail with assorted Hamlet-type costumes and
   Jameson's Ophelia underslip
2 large cushions (in hamper)
2 shuttlecocks (Jameson)

Congo props: Blunderbuss (Dean)
                African mask & carpet beater (Brown)
                Indian head-dress & 2 hair brushes (Patterson)
                Indian head-dress, large shield & spear with forked
                    end (Butler)
                Mask & Tomahawk (Robinson)
                Shield, spear & mask (Mckenna)
                Indian head-dress, bow, maracas & arrows
                    (Richards)
                Leopard sash, mask, bass drum & drumsticks
                    (Lowry)

4 cards (with Bill Dunham's speech)
4 sherry glasses (with sherry)
'Bawdy' text book (Jameson)
Small suitcase (Barry)

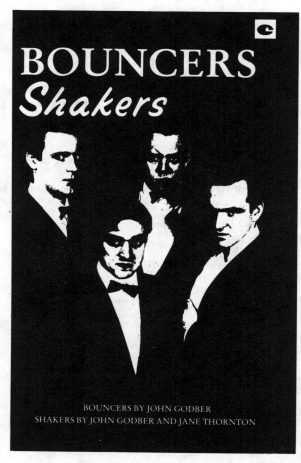

BOUNCERS
Shakers

BOUNCERS BY JOHN GODBER
SHAKERS BY JOHN GODBER AND JANE THORNTON

Bouncers and Shakers, a volume of two plays, now available from Chappell Plays.

It's Friday night, it's disco night — time for 'bouncers' to come alive! In this outrageous and hilarious parody of the contemporary disco scene, four brutish bouncers portraying over twenty different characters invite us for a night out on the town. Join them on the disco floor where the pulsating beat and flashing lights mesmerize the groovers. "Brilliant . . . consistently entertaining" *Evening Standard*

Shakers is the local trendy cocktail bar where everyone wants to be seen: from the check-out girls to the chinless wonders, the yuppies to the local lads tittering at the thought of a 'Long Slow Comfortable Screw'. We are given a wickedly funny glimpse of this world by four waitresses who offer a fascinating view of the reality that lurks behind the plastic palms and Pina Coladas.

For further information, contact Chappell Plays Ltd, 129 Park Street, London W1Y 3FA. Telephone 01-629 7600.